I0014656

Internet of Things

Building Predictive Maintenance Systems

(Your Guide to the Connected Future and Programming Digital Circuits With Python)

Jose Blevins

Published By **Regina Loviusher**

Jose Blevins

Internet of Things: Building Predictive Maintenance Systems (Your Guide to the Connected Future and Programming Digital Circuits With Python)

ISBN 978-1-990373-96-1

No part of this guidebook shall be reproduced in any form without permission in writing from the publisher except in the case of brief quotations embodied in critical articles or reviews.

Legal & Disclaimer

The information contained in this book is not designed to replace or take the place of any form of medicine or professional medical advice. The information in this book has been provided for educational & entertainment purposes only.

The information contained in this book has been compiled from sources deemed reliable, and it is accurate to the best of the Author's knowledge; however, the Author cannot guarantee its accuracy and validity and cannot be held liable for any errors or omissions. Changes are periodically made to this book. You must consult your doctor or get professional medical advice before using any of the suggested remedies, techniques, or information in this book.

Table Of Contents

Chapter 1: Extreme Iot Execution Guide For Organizations

IoT will bring numerous benefits to the company; but, it could be a challenge to carry out. Learn about the requirements and apply the most effective practices to ensure the most efficient arrangement.

The web of things offers organizations continuous data and this is the kind of data that business encounters that are followed-up on and analyzed, will eventually help them become more efficient. IT Directors, engineers, and designers and CIOs who are considering the possibility of a web of thing arrangement must have a thorough understanding of what the internet of things is, how it works, ways it functions and its purpose, requirements for tradeoffs, as well as how to manage the web of things with gadgets and the foundations.

What is IoT?

The Internet of Things (IoT) is a collection that is comprised of devices called objects - that are sent as a way to gather and exchange authentic information over the web, or with different businesses. The examples of this innovative action include the following:

Patients with a heart condition are fitted with a heart sensor during a medical procedure reporting symptomatic details about every patient's heart to a observing physician.

Sensors are used in homes for projects like security as well as house administration, for example machines, lighting and lights and status information and controls made through cellphone applications.

Dampness sensors are used by ranchers across the entire field to help coordinate the system of water to maximize yields in the areas that require it.

Farmers employ areas sensors that are placed on each steer's head to help distinguish and locate dairy cows on the farm.

The modern workplace uses sensors to monitor the existence of potentially hazardous substances or working conditions. They also monitor the development of workers throughout the workplace.

The urban areas use an array of sensors to monitor traffic and street circumstances, adjusting a traffic signal's mechanical system progressively according to its course, and also smoothing traffic to reflect the most favorable circumstances.

Principal ideas behind IoT can be described as follows: below:

A focus on authentic data. In cases where an organization regularly has to manage files, slideshows, photographs and recordings, calculator sheets, as well as a variety of kinds of complex static information, IoT equipment produces information that usually reflects at the very the very least one aspect real. IoT devices can aid a company in understanding the state of affairs, but additionally make it easier to control what's happening.

The crucial importance of rapidity and swiftly advancing the activity. In cases where routine information, for instance, a reminder file can be stored for a period of time, if not months and it is not used, IoT gadgets should convey data for handling and aggregation quickly. The underlying factors such as the capacity of transmission for an organization as well as network capacity, crucial to IoT situations.

The following information by in itself. IoT projects are usually defined by the larger purpose or the business motive driving IoT organizations. The majority of the time, IoT information is essential to create a control circle that is characterized by clear conditions and an clear results. In this instance, a sensor will inform a home owner that their front entrance is open, while the owner of the mortgage can make use of an actuator. It's an IoT device designed to convert commands from an company into actual activities and then securely lock it remotely.

But, IoT can uphold a greater and wider range of commercial goals. Many IoT sensors are capable of creating massive amounts of data - which is a huge amount of information that people can audit and then follow-up on. Gradually, huge IoT projects form the basis of massive information-driven drives, such as, AI (ML) and man-made conscious (AI) project. Information gathered by huge IoT devices can be processed and analyzed for making fundamental business projections or build AI frameworks based on actual data collected from massive sensor clusters. The back-end analysis can demand large amounts of capacity and register energy. Registration can be handled by concentrating server farms transparently mists or distributed through a small number of edge regions of figuring where data is collected.

What is the function of IoT work?

IoT isn't one gadget, programmer or ingenuity. IoT can be described as a mix of devices, companies that can be used to calculate assets as well as stacks of programming tools and instruments. It is important to understand IoT terminology usually begins with the IoT devices.

Things. Every IoT device - also known as a gadget or an amazing sensor is an incredibly committed PC with an embedded processor, firmware, as well as a the ability to limit memory and network for organization. The device collects precise data and then sends it to an organization that uses IP similar to the internet. Based on the sensors' work and capabilities, it can also include channels, intensifiers as well as converters. IoT gadgets run on batteries and rely on remote organisation connectivity via IP addresses. IoT gadgets are designed by themselves or as part of a group.

Associations. The data collected from IoT devices should be transmitted and collected. The 2nd layer of IoT encompasses the large network, as well as a connecting to the company and the back-end processing. It is typically an ordinary network that is based on IP, similar to an Ethernet LAN or the web. Every IoT gadget is assigned a distinctive IP address as well as a unique identification number. The information it transmits to an enterprise via the remote organizational interface such as Wi-Fi, or cell-based organization like 5G or 4G. In the same way, for any business device, data bundles are separated by an unambiguous IP address to which the information will be directed and transferred. The information transfer of organizations is not different from regular exchange of information from an organization among standard computers. This crude sensor information is typically an intermediary connection point, such as IoT center or IoT centre or IoT entrance. IoT entryways are IoT doorway, for majority of the time, is used to collect and analyze the sensors' raw data. This is usually done by making use of early processing assignments that include standardization, as well as segregating the IoT data.

Back-end. The huge amount of data generated by the IoT sensor and then gathered through the IoT entryway must be separated into smaller pieces of data, like finding business's incredible open doors, as well as driving AI. The IoT entrance sends clean and tied-down sensor data over the internet to an back-end for processing and analysis. Investigative tasks are carried out using broad processing groups like, Hadoop bunches. The backend could be located in a corporation server farm, colocation office, or even a modeling framework that is built within the public cloud. In the cloud, data is stored, processed in a manner that is displayed and analyzed.

What are the different layers in the IoT design?

The conversations between a sensor as well as association and layers behind the scenes can aid companies, as well as IT by utilizing staffing to gain IoT innovations, however this conversations also require a consideration of IoT designs. Although the extent and details of IoT structure IoT structure can vary dramatically, dependent on the IoT initiative, innovators need to be thinking about the way IoT integrates into this IT basis.

Four major engineering problems:

1. Foundation. The layer itself comprises IoT devices, the company as well as figuring resources utilized to process the data. The

framework conversation typically includes the types of sensors, their amounts of areas, energy, networks points of contact and arrangement as well as the executive's tools. The networks include capacity for data transfer and idleness considerations in order to make sure that they're able to deal with IoT device request. Registering is the process of analyzing the back. Likewise, associations might need to transfer information assets that can handle additional handling, or utilize on-demand resources, such as the cloud. Foundation conversations also contain the consideration of IoT rules and conventions such as Bluetooth, GSM, 4G or 5G, Wi-Fi Zigbee and the Low-Power Wireless Personal area Network.

2. Security. Information transmitted via the internet of things could be tangled and classified. Sharing such data across public organizations could reveal gadgets and data that can be used to evade detection or

hacking. Organizations that are planning the IoT project need to think about the best strategies to keep IoT devices and data flying and in a very quiet. The use of encryption is the most common method used to secure IoT security of information. Additional security must be added to IoT devices to avoid hackers and harmful modifications to the design of devices. Security encompasses a variety of programming tools and standard security tools, including firewalls and interruption detection as well as anticipation frameworks.

3. Mix. Mix is a mix of everything working seamlessly, making sure that the equipment that are used as foundations, devices, and other equipment that are added to IoT are compatible with the existing frameworks and software similar to frameworks used by executives use and ERP that are set by the group. The proper coordination demands careful planning and verification of the rule-

testing along with a thorough assessment of IoT platforms and devices, for example, Apache Kafka or OpenRemote.

4. Analyzing and showing. The ultimate goal of an IoT concept requires a clear knowledge of the way IoT data will be analyzed and used. The app layer, which typically includes scientific equipment, AI, and ML making motors, demonstrating them and the representation of devices. These tools can be purchased through outside retailers or by cloud providers where data is stored and managed.

Case studies for business use in IoT

The wide array of tiny and versatile IoT devices has led to important business applications within large companies. Consider a few of the growing application scenarios in five important companies:

1. Home (business or final client). IoT gadgets are spotted at homes to provide

energy for executive, security as well as, perhaps, task mechanization

The indoor lighting and regulators can be controlled and booked via web-based applications.

Motion-initiated sensors are able to trigger sound and video transmits to mobile phones.

Sensors for water can monitor the storm cellars for leaks.

Fire, smoke, and CO_2 detectors can be used to identify risks for clients.

IoT actuators are able to be used to lock and unlock entryways at an extended distance.

The smart coolers are able to monitor contents, while computerized vacuums clean the house without the need for human intervention.

2. Producing. IoT gadgets have discovered wide-ranging reception in all kinds of

assembly and contemporary setting. The modern internet of objects (IIoT) include the following:

IoT labels are able to follow to locate and store the resources needed to complete an undertaking.

IoT gadgets are able to help monitor and optimize the use of energy. This includes, for instance dimming lighting levels during times when the human-occupied areas are not in use or decreasing temperature settings when it is not in use.

IoT sensors and actuators could ensure that processes are computerized and improved.

IoT devices are able to monitor an array of ways that machines behave and defining boundaries in normal activity and enabling ML to provide prescient advice on maintenance to improve cycle efficiency.

3. General (wellbeing and security). IoT sensors that have cell class connectivity can

collaborate with metropolitan areas to meet many needs:

IoT gadgets are able to detect the presence of traffic and allow urban areas to modify the lighting of roads that are not in use as well as off-hours.

The wrongdoing of anticipation activities may involve camera-based surveillance, and an associated sound spot could direct officers to areas that are prone to gunfire.

Cameras are able in order to improve and control the flow of traffic. Transponders and cameras are able to peruse tags and cost boxes to help coordinate price assortment as well as the board.

Interconnected stop frameworks enable urban areas to track parking spots and guide drivers for parking spaces that are accessible through applications.

Sensors monitor various constructions as well as spans, for issues and stress which allows for early detection and the ability to correct.

Sensors may be used to monitor the water's quality and enable to detect toxic substances and foreign chemicals.

4. Health and wellness. IoT is accessible to remote permanent telemetry, as well as for other medical reasons:

IoT is accessible with incalculable wearable remote gadgets such as the pulse sleeves and screens and the glucometer. Gadgets can be adjusted to detect the amount of calories consumed, objectives for practicing as well as assist patients in keep track of prescriptions and arrangements.

IoT allows early warning devices such as fall recognition that can notify health professionals and family members and provide location information to anticipate the situation.

Remote observing from IoT helps wellbeing providers in monitoring patient health and adhering to treatments as well as assisting in connecting health issues to telemetry data.

Clinics may use IoT tags to track the ongoing field of equipment used in clinical settings, like oxygen defibrillators, nebulizers and defibrill and wheelchairs.

IoT for identification of staff members can assist in finding and directing employees much more efficiently.

IoT could assist in different gear controls - for instance, stock at the drugstore as well as cooler temperatures and Mugginess control and temperature control.

The IoT's cleanliness monitoring equipment helps in ensuring the clinical environment is perfect and can aid in decreasing the incidence of illness.

5. Retail. IoT and massive information analysis have been able to track the use of IoT for retail offers and condition of stores:

IoT devices are able to label every item to enable computers to control stock, make the ability to predict misfortune, and on the network - making orders visible to the current deals and inventory levels.

Cameras and other advances can monitor customer actions and movements, assisting stores improve design and align related products in order to increase sales.

IoT devices are able to support check-outs that are touchless, without examination and installments, for instance in relation to managing the installment of correspondence.

What are the advantages for businesses from IoT?

If a business is the first to study and think about IoT reception, easy to see records mention the benefits of IoT including more effective operations and longer-lasting cost investments. Although this may be true but these debates are mostly disorienting from the main benefits of IoT the information and understanding.

Quick and simple decisions require details and information that could be problematic or difficult to obtain. Companies attempt to acquire the knowledge and information and use it every time someone in the project leads evaluates the next quarter's earnings or creative director decides when to shut down an important machine on an essential production line to ensure routine maintenance. There are greater stakes in the event that state control officers discover problems in the long neglected medical foundations or fights to keep a developing health-care patient safe.

IoT provides more immediate data by estimating and showing the truthful circumstances. It's cutting-edge instrumentation. It is able to be analysed and addressed constantly. If an alarming pulse is displayed, warning of unneeded pulses the patient is able to adjust the dial or unwind it to lower the level of pulse to an acceptable level. use a medication that is appropriate and then contact their doctor to seek additional guidance or seek medical assistance. If a traffic-checking framework is able to detect a resurgence of a major interstate, it may make travel plans more flexible to the typical situations, and enable suburbs to pick alternate ways to travel and avoid from a clog.

The real strength and benefit of IoT are the lengthy experience it offers to entrepreneurs. Take a look at the countless IoT sensors that are transmitted through various hardware structures, vehicles and other civil zones which enable better long-term understanding through the use of cutting-edge analysis - including the back-end figuring process is suited to evaluate and translate huge amounts of insignificant data to answer queries from businesses and create precise forecasts of future events. Data gathered from sensors can be used to create ML models that support the development of AI drives which provide an extensive understanding of details and their relationships.

As an example, the shift sensors that are used in modern device can be dissected to detect different kinds of inactivity or condition. This could suggest the need for maintenance or anticipate the onset of a loss. These bits of information allow businesses to organize items, arrange support or fix issues in a proactive manner, while also limiting the disruption to routine work.

Chapter 2: What Are The Challenges Of Iot?

IoT initiatives can provide significant positive benefits for businesses, regardless of the extension. But, IoT can likewise present serious challenges for businesses that they needs to be aware of before launching any IoT initiative.

Plan of action. Even though it is true that IoT devices are able to quickly implement various guidelines like 5G or Wi-Fi however, at present there are no universally accepted guidelines that define the design and operation of IoT designs - and there's no set of rules to guide the way of the best way to approach to an IoT project. This is because it takes into consideration an abundance of flexibility in the plan, but also takes into account significant flaws in the plan as well as oversights. IoT activities should be, in the majority of cases run by IT personnel equipped with IoT expertise, however this expertise evolves daily. In the end, there's only one option that is careful, well-thought out strategy and demonstrated execution due to the overwhelming testing and verifying of guideline initiatives.

Maintenance and capacity for information. IoT devices generate huge amounts of information that can be quickly replicated due to the sheer number of devices in the system. This information is an important source of information for businesses that must be stored and accessible. In addition, unlike typical business data, such as messages or contracts, IoT information is profoundly sensitive to time. As an example, the car's speed, or road information that were published yesterday or in the last month might not apply in the present or a year down the road. It is conceivable that IoT information may have an extremely unique lifecycle compared to traditional business-related information. This is why it's important to set a significant interest to limit the amount of information that can be accessed, as well as security and a lifecycle of information to the executive.

Support for networks. IoT data should be transferred across any IP company, for example either a LAN or public internet. Consider the effect of IoT devices on speed of transfer across networks and ensure that adequate secure information transmission is available. Blocks with dropped packets or high levels of dormancy could delay the transfer of IoT data. This may involve a couple of modifications to the structure and expansion of networks that are committed. In other words, rather than being able to pass the entire IoT data across the internet businesses could choose to share an edge-figuring engineering system that stores and processes local to the information before transferring the arranged data to an location for further investigation.

Gadgets and security of information. IoT gadgets are tiny PCs that are part of a normal business, rendering them unprotected against robbery and hacking. IoT initiatives should implement security measures to protect devices including information on-flight and the information that's in-flight. The legitimate and thoroughly planned IoT security posture will have implications on compliance with the administrative system.

Gadget the CEOs. Another issue that's often ignored is the ad-hoc proliferation of IoT devices. Every IoT device should be purchased prepared, connected, introduced, organized as needed, backed on top of, and finally replaced or retired. It's one thing managing the management of a handful of servers. It's another managing hundreds, thousands or perhaps millions of IoT gadgets. Think about the massive chaos that comes with changing batteries for numerous remote IoT devices. IoT innovators must use tools that monitor IoT devices from the beginning of their designing and arrangement to check regular support, as well as manner of operation.

Security and consistency of IoT

The business and IT leaders should be aware of the importance of security and scalability in any IoT arrangement. IoT gadgets have similar security vulnerabilities that can be found on any well-organized PC. The problem that IoT gadgets face IoT is the volume of:

Certain IoT devices may not be aware of an entire set of security features or implement ineffective security standards, such as there is no standard secret word.

There could be tens, or perhaps a plethora of IoT devices that are connected to an IoT sending device - each with the same expected flaws.

IT professionals should make use of tools that are suited to finding, organizing and evaluating the functionality of all IoT devices in the transmitting.

Every IoT device should be designed to make use of the most solid security features.

IoT security could pose a problem for businesses due to the fact that security defaults are ineffective and enhanced by the endless number of devices which all depend on humans observing as well as the board's initiatives. The attack surface could be huge. In this sense, IoT security is boiled down to three fundamental concerns:

Plan. I will select IoT devices with the most solid security options that are easily accessible and available.

Process. It used methods, instruments and techniques that successfully identify and design the best IoT device, which includes device firmware updates when they are accessible.

Steadiness. We use tools for securing and implementing IoT gadget configurations, as well as security devices that are able to detect the presence of malware or interruptions in IoT device configurations.

However, IoT devices are afflicted by the possibility of destroying attacks that include botnets and weak DNS structures that permit the transmission of malware ransomware and other attack routes triggered by untested or unstable devices that are a threat to an organization and, shockingly, the risk from actual security.

Security has the chance to communicate relating risks to an organization's consistent act. Imagine what could happen if data from patients is retrieved from the clinical IoT foundation or firm isn't able to create items due to hackers have infected the IoT framework by introducing ransomware. These scenarios could cause problems for pioneers of business and controllers. Every discussion concerning IoT security needs to include an examination of the the consistency.

IoT is not yet fully developed. There isn't any standard universally accepted guidelines to plan, organize work, or establishing an IoT base. In the end all that's left is to document your cycle and plan options and try to link these with different IT top techniques. A good way to start is by choosing IoT products that conform to the current mechanical standards such as IPv6 as well as network concepts such as Bluetooth Low Energy, Wi-Fi, Thread, Zigbee, and Z-Wave. It's an excellent start however, it's often not enough.

There is good news that additional consistency standards emerge from organizations that drive industry, such as the IEEE. IEEE 2413-2019 is the IEEE Standard for an Architectural Framework for IoT. It provides a standard arrangement that can be used for IoT that spans medical, transportation utility, as well as other locations. It is adapted to the international standard ISO/IEC/IEEE42010:2011. While these standards don't guarantee the sameness without any other organisations that adhere to the plan's structures and procedures can strengthen existing consistency standards in IoT implementation.

IoT managements and plans of actions

Getting a variety of IoT gadgets installed can be a daunting task However, navigating this information in order to discover useful information for business could bring challenges and challenges. As the IoT technology grows it is becoming more complex. IoT setting is growing to offer new support to IoT implementation, and also to develop innovative plans for implementation.

The most important issue that comes that I have encountered with IoT is that it absolutely inspires it to perform.

Foundation demands can be rather vast, security may be difficult, and the handling of it can make it more complicated for the company. IoT sellers are working to resolve the issue with an increasing range of SaaS platforms that aim to enhance IoT reception, and eliminate a lot of complicated speculations that typically are necessary for passages, edge calculation, and various other IoT explicit elements.

IoT SaaS works between the IoT gadget field as well as the business. SaaS manages a wide range of essential components the venture should be able to offer. In particular that the SaaS service typically handles the simplest projects within the framework such as announcements and security of information. But, as it happens however, the SaaS service will typically include a significant portion of the top level handling and registration, such as investigations, as well as support in ML. It shields the effort server farm from IoT issue, and also businesses can focus to obtaining and using further investigations.

IoT SaaS contributions give comparative aspects, therefore you should carefully take a look at the assessment to pick the best one according for the number of IoT devices, data volumes as well as the needs of your organization. Common IoT SaaS suppliers incorporate Altair SmartWorks, EMnify, Google Cloud IoT Core, IBM Watson IoT Platform, Microsoft Azure IoT Hub as well as Oracle IoT.

IoT has not just impacted the way that companies operate. It's creating a range of fresh strategies that allow companies earn revenue through IoT projects and products. There's a range of four types of strategies which IoT could work with:

1. Marketing-ready information. The basic information gathered through IoT devices can be quickly modified. As an example, the information collected by an individual

health tracker could be intriguing for medical insurance companies looking to adjust rates, based on health of the buyer.

2. Business-to-business and business-to-purchaser. IoT can be linked to the collection and breakdown of data, and this research is a great way to identify the brand's loyalty and increase it, and drive more offers in light of the needs of business or shoppers that are distinguished by IoT equipment.

3. IoT stage. Information and research gathered through IoT can be the basis of stages which offer AI management such as Alexa. The stages are able to continue learning and grow as well as the services offered are able to be utilized by other organisations at an additional cost.

4. Pay-per-use. Companies, such as bicycle rentals or bikes can be quickly facilitated through IoT advancements where equipment can be tracked through GPS and

accessed by customers using related applications. Then, the hardware is was used, and then paid for. IoT data can be used to analyze the use of a device and provide examples of support in order to improve the efficiency of business.

What are the requirements to implement IoT?

There are a variety of specialized concerns related to IoT that include the choice and configuration of equipment as well as the availability of networks, developing scientific capabilities that are adequate and meet limitations. However, the variety of thoughts is connected to the real structure and function of the IoT structure. In some organizations, the basic questions are much simpler; the reason why and where do we start?

Similar to any IT initiative like any other IT-related project IoT project should start by using a method that outlines the purpose for the project and clearly articulates the goals. This kind of approach can also highlight the intended benefit - for instance, increased effectiveness or reduced costs due to meticulous maintenance - - of the project to justify the academic and financial hypothesis that is necessary.

As a result of a process that is in place, the company generally goes into an era of testing as well as trial and error in order to determine IoT elements, software as well as other components of the framework. Directors of projects then conduct limited verification of the standard projects to demonstrate the new technology and improve its structure and its board-level strategies, including setting up and security. In parallel, they evaluate methods using the data as well as understanding the gadgets, and the figuring framework that is expected to gain business insight of the IoT data. This may include using limited servers farm resources for narrow range examination with the eye on public cloud administration and assets when the IoT project expands.

The business may move towards the IoT project through three different ways:

1. It could be an exploratory task that involves gathering an area and helping clients find their esteem.

2. The task could be more formalized, using distinct task diagrams and a timetable for the undertaking.

3. It could be a matter of addressing an entire obligation to IoT throughout the organization However, this type of job usually requires greater skill and confidence with respect to IoT as compared to other.

However you choose to approach it you choose, it is important to remain focused on the value IoT can bring to your business.

What are the potential risks and challenges of implementing IoT?

While the potential dangers are generally speaking already known however, the massive amount and diversity of IoT devices require a greater extensive level of attention and oversight than any business may be in some way. Some of the most imminent dangers associated with IoT circumstances include:

Inability to locate the entire array of IoT devices. IoT devices and rehearsals are required to be able to locate and placing every IoT devices within the climate. The gadgets that are not visible to the eye aren't managed which could be a source of attack that allow programmers to access the business. From a wider perspective administrators must have the ability to locate and manage all devices in the business.

Access control is not always correct or has been lost. control. IoT security is dependent on the proper validation and authorization of each device. It is bolstered by each device's unique identifier, but it is still essential to organize every IoT gadget to the smallest degree of respect - and focusing on only the assets of your organization which are essential. Create other safety measures through embracing strong passwords and making it possible to enable network encryption on every IoT device.

• Disregarded or ignored gadget refreshes. IoT devices may require periodic adjustments or changes to the internal software or firmware. Inattention or disregarding an updates can make IoT devices unable to withstand interruption or hacking. Be aware of updating techniques and methods when designing your IoT weather condition. Some devices may prove problematic or difficult to refresh on the spot and may even be restricted or dangerous to use disconnected.

• Poor or inadequate security for the company. IoT businesses can include an array of devices in a networking. Each gadget creates the possibility of interruption. Companies that use IoT often carry out additional security measures for the entire organization, such as Counteraction and interruption-detection structures, tightly controlled firewalls and robust anti-malware software. They can also choose to separate the IoT network in the same way as other parts of the IT company.

• Absence of a safety strategy or cycle. Strategies and interactions are essential in ensuring that the security of your organization is adequate. This is the mix of practices and tools that are used to create, monitor and ensure the security of gadgets within the enterprise. Documentation that is accurate, well-defined arrangement guidelines, and rapid detailing as well as quick reaction are crucial to ensure IoT as well as normal security of the organization.

Developments and ventures for execution

There's not a single universal method of creating and running the IoT basis. There are a common set of considerations that could aid organizations in taking a look at all the boxes to accurately design and submit the IoT project. The most important execution thoughts include the following:

Network availability. IoT devices can provide a number of options for networks such as Wi-Fi Bluetooth, 4G, and 5G. There isn't a standard for every device to have the same network, but using a standard approach could be a good idea for gadget configuration as well as analyzing. In addition, decide if sensors and actuators should use the same organization, or another.

IoT the center of. The idea is to pass the entire IoT information directly from devices to an investigative stage could result in unique connections as well as a lackluster display. An intermediate stage, such as the IoT center point, could assist in separating, processing and relay information from devices throughout an area before transmitting that data to an analysis. In the event that a remote office is IoT enabled, a central point is able to preprocess and assemble this IoT data on the edge before transferring it for further analysis.

Investigation and accumulation. Once the data is collected the data could be used to drive announcement mechanisms and actuators or be gathered to conduct a more thorough research, inquiry, and various other information-related purposes. Decide on the tools utilized to process the data, break it down, think about and create models of ML. One model takes into account the selection of IoT information bases and data set structure -- SQL against NoSQL or static, as opposed streaming. They can also be connected to the local server farm or accessed via SaaS or cloud-based providers.

• Gadget board as well as control. Use a tool that's which is able to consistently adjust each of the IoT devices throughout the IoT project's lifespan. Find higher degrees of automation and collect the abilities of the CEO to improve design and minimize errors. IoT device fixing and refreshing is a growing issue organizations should be attentive to revamping and refreshing the processes of work.

Security. Every IoT device could be a security flaw, and therefore any IoT deployment should be accompanied by the utmost care in IoT arrangement, and its integration with the existing security tools and stages (like interruption avoidance and discovery frameworks as well as antimalware tools).

What's the future of IoT?

The future of IoT could be difficult to predict given that IoT's technology and applications are only a little bit fresh and possess huge growth potential. However there are the most basic of predictions.

IoT devices are growing. The next couple of years will witness billions of additional IoT devices added on the web. They will be augmented with the latest innovations that include 5G connectivity and a myriad of instances of business applications that arise in major ventures like healthcare and the assembling of.

The coming years will also witness a revision and growth of IoT security. This will start by establishing a plan for the initial gadget, and then the business decision and implementation. The future gadgets will be joined by more established security features that are incorporated by the standard. Security tools that are already in place, such as instance, interrupt recognition and anticipation, are set to include aid with IoT systems with comprehensive recording and dynamic remediation. Additionally, IoT gadgets and the executive's devices will be gradually emphasized in the importance of security assessment and will naturally tackle IoT devices' security issues.

In the end, IoT information volumes will continue to grow and transform to new revenues and open doors to businesses. This information will gradually create ML and AI operations across a variety of enterprises that span from transportation to science and financing to retail.

Chapter 3: What Are The Internet Of Things' Business Advantages?

How Does the Internet of Things (IoT) Help Businesses?

IoT can change the ways businesses work and interact with their clients. Learn the ways IoT can help businesses extend their reach and streamline tasks to meet the best primary goal.

The Global IoT Business Opportunity

IoT uses tech connectivity to help advance the technology of computerized change. In recent times, IoT reception has soared across all industries.

The IoT market is expected to grow to over $1300 billion before 2026. It's predicted to bring in the equivalent of $4-11 trillion in value over the same period.

The Internet of Things has created many new possibilities to grow and develop. In reality, 83% of companies who have implemented IoT innovations have improved their capabilities.

Realizing the numerous benefits of IoT technology The business community is increasingly investing resources in IoT technology:

Over 80% of all gathering organizations plan to invest money in IoT

90percent of retailers are planning to make use of the Internet of Things to modify the store-specific information

95% of senior leaders in the fields of media, technology and telecom view IoT as essential to the growth of the industry.

What Business Benefits Does the Internet of Things Provide?

It is more likely that you have were aware that information is the latest oil.

In the age of IoT advancements, your business will be able to use every datum use to achieve development goals as well as improve the efficiency of procedures. Below are some examples of what using the Internet of Things might help your company

IoT aids businesses in reducing costs

IoT arrangement smooths out current routines in the assembling process, inventory network creating, and various projects. The smoothed-out processes limit vacation time and reduce expenses.

The assembly business provides an excellent example of cost savings through the application of IoT technology.

Manufacturing facilities employ advanced support technologies to reduce holidays by as much as 20-half and also save between 5-10% on cost of maintenance.

IoT helps improve efficiency and profit.

IoT allows for advanced workflow procedures possible through automation. It helps to reduce the burden of assignments, and is able to make the most efficient making use of assets that are accessible as well as hardware.

Improved efficiency prevents wasted time in organizations which makes the activities more effective.

The truth is that 83% of companies that are fueled by IoT will reduce their consumption, and improve the efficiency of employees. A analysis of Aruba discovered that 75% of companies adopting IoT increased their efficiency.

IoT uncovers new business open doors.

IoT integrates programming, equipment with computer-generated reasoning to enable an even deeper investigation. With the aim of providing better experiences businesses can make use of IoT in order to move their work in the direction of the next.

36% of companies discover new doors to open with IoT.

Organisations create new products and income model in light the new trends.

As an example, backup plans determine expenses by analyzing the driving habits of customers. Retailers design their stock level and their in-store display by recording the conduct of their customers. Advertisers make use of IoT-based guide technology to collect information regarding shoppers. Information analysis assists companies with changing their strategies and creating products that are market ready.

IoT helps to improve the use of resources and follows.

IoT will connect each device such as a gadget, device, resource equipment, or hardware to an unified company. Through smart sensors, companies are able to track devices and resources. Regular experiences and a centralized management reduce waste and enhance all aspects of the process. Transportation companies that are resource-intensive make use of IoT to enhance the ease of working in this area by implementing updates and monitoring.

IoT enhances security and reduces weaknesses

IoT helps reduce security threats and vulnerabilities through sensors designed to be live-streamed in real zones.

The integration of CCTV cameras into IoT networks creates a robust surveillance organization. It can also be enhanced with the help of computers, deep learning and computer vision, to design customized security plans. In particular, ALERTWildfire, another AI recognition company that is proving to be increasingly accurate in predicting fires that are out of control.

What is the way IoT helps businesses across Different Industries?

IoT technology is helping businesses to collect and process additional information to improve user experience. There are additional applications too. Here are some instances of the ways in which IoT works in various industries:

Modern art and creation, assembling

The area of assembly has undergone an enormous change due to IoT and the computerization. The most advanced sensors boost effectiveness and decrease personal time through an array of arrangements that go with it:

Independent creation units

Modern robots powered by IoT reduce the mishaps caused by negligence of humans. Additionally, they can be employed throughout the day, every single minute. They increase the production yield, as well as assist with decreasing the cost of their work.

The independent units are controlled remotely to create sequential systems that can be used for the production of a broad range of objects. Worldwide, automotive, mechanical parts, toys and even planes are manufactured using IoT also known as it's the Internet of Robotic Things (IoT) for short.

Prescient upkeep

IoT sensors are able to monitor the wellbeing of gears continuously. The data gathered by IoT generates upkeep schedules that are intermittent which do not affect the efficiency of production lines.

Additionally, it helps administrators identify requirements for support well in advance of the time. IoT sensors predict the possibility of disappointment with gear for updated support plans. These forecasts are able to reduce the effect a failure has on the dynamic hours of creation.

Massive facilities use associated sensors for enhancing upkeep plans. For instance, take Volvo for example and the business uses IoT to monitor hardware failures and anticipate upkeep plans. This results in a 70 percent reduction in the time to diagnose and a 20% reduction on fix times.

Network of production and coordination

Networks of production and co-ordinated operations are typically business that are capital-expanding, and have a lot of obstructions. The clients require reliability as well as organizations are required to operate more efficiently. IoT helps organizations achieve the following two goals:

Global positioning frameworks that are more effective

Customers appreciate having a thorough knowledge of their packages right at the time they send the request. IoT-based packages provide point-by-point information concerning the present situation for the product to delight and entice buyers.

The parcel uses IoT to provide continuous information regarding the condition of a parcel. Transporters and providers can provide the most important customer assistance as well as a brief goals for questions.

In the case of high-end merchandise such as perishables or temperature sensitive products like immunizations IoT sensors are crucial in providing basic information on components such as dampness, temperature and more.

Pick-up on-request and transport

The clients love the comfort. This is especially true when it is able to fix a problem area.

Brilliant Get focuses on assisting with the planning and transportation activities to the internet-based business sector. As an example, companies could benefit from an organizational structure of storage space that is connected to the Internet of Things to transport products. The storage facilities are linked with the web and notify the customers whenever a package shows up.

One of our IoT projects, Collectomate, we made the process of transferring bundles easier for customers who work in large workplaces. Users use portable applications to access their storage space at an appropriate timing. There's no need to leave important gatherings, or worry about losing their delivery should they be unavailable to pick up the delivery.

Collectorate uses IoT to provide amazing conveyances as well as improving the bundle pickup process in huge workplaces. Learn the ways Collectomate improves the conveyance of bundles in huge workplaces.

Advancement of the course and mileage

Frameworks built with IoT can help managers reduce the costs of their tasks through streamlining the programs. Organisations are able to design effective conveyance programs for efficient transports by using driver conduct environmental stewardship, as well as support the expectations of their customers.

Investigating and following reduces expenses and also track problems such as individual vehicle use by employees.

Medical care

Specialists and clinics use IoT to monitor patients and provide prevention-based medical care. IoT is a tool that can help make informed decisions in the treatment and analytic process. burns. It's as simple as:

Monitoring of wellbeing via the internet

IoT devices can track fundamental health indicators like blood sugar levels, pulses blood pressure, circulation strain and many more. Doctors can get detailed information on an individual's health through equipment equipped with sophisticated sensors.

Medical workers make use of this technology to look out for patients on a regular basis.

The advancing technology of IoT gadgets has helped the business of telemedicine. The arrangements such as TeleICU are able to make precise predictions about the health of patients. The calculations analyze the data gathered through IoT and can predict the time when patients will need urgent medical supervision.

Media creation

IoT can also be a useful technology in creative ventures such as media and production. It is believed that the Internet of Things can make the process of creation more effective and active.

Computerization of the on-set climate

Making the proper lighting to create video is a complicated and intricate procedure. IoT is able to work with changes in light and enable gaffers to control lighting devices via cellphones.

The Lighticians Apollo Control interfaces with all lighting equipment using DMX. Light experts as well as novices are able to instantly set up their lighting scenes and analyze the moment-specific details of light.

Farming

In recent times, agribusiness has experienced the rise of interconnected agreements that allow ranchers to stay more in control of their present circumstances.

Independent cultivating gear

In this case, John Deere has a collection of products for measuring important rural components. Collecting soil temperatures, dampness levels and air temperature as well as the speed of wind provide ranchers with valuable information.

WEB OF THINGS IN BUSINESS

In the business world that are in the business of acquiring,"the" Internet of Things means a variety of items

Do With It

It is the Internet of Things (IoT) is the continuously evolving assortment of devices ranging from mobile phones to sensors-equipped robots for assembly - connected via the internet. Through this connectivity that they have, they are able to transmit and receive information, which is a capability that can be used in a variety of tasks in everyday life and the business. IoT is widely recognized in the sense that, in 2025, researchers from the International Data Corporation (IDC) expect that over 55.7 billion connected devices will be operating in the business center. the majority of them being associated to the IoT level.

IoT is now an essential component of many working environments. What ever your business is, there's an possibility to use IoT devices to play some role in the outcomes of your company. It doesn't matter if you're using a simple like bright lights to create a comfortable office environment or something more intricate such as an arrangement that makes use of advanced machines to detect the quality issues that arise during the assembling process, IoT is there.

What Is IoT?

IoT is a broad term which refers to a variety of devices that are connected to the internet. They can include everything of them, from delivery addresses as well as speakers, to cars as well as planes. They can include sophisticated sensors, lighting as well as security systems, along with massive modern devices and other devices that feed information back to the internet and integrate in conjunction with it. Also, there's another option, the Industrial Internet of Things (IIoT) it is an acronym for similar requirements but can also be utilized for business purposes and devices such as an element of hardware that can be assembled.

What is the reason why IoT crucial for companies? IoT is a business tool that can have different forms, but the majority of it involves gathering data about processes, conduct as well as other situations. Many IoT devices also require longer time to analyze the issue, make improvements, or in case they don't, make use of these data to implement any kind of improvement. The possibilities are endless as well as the benefits of IoT are gaining momentum.

The Beneficial Impact of IoT on Businesses

In light of the explosion of IoT-related devices, you might be wondering, "How does IoT influence business?" It's simple "Inside and out."

The accessibility to huge informational databases, along with the free exchange and distribution of data, means that it's becoming easier to gain experience regarding things such as client manners to behave and the execution of products. IoT also aids in continuous improvement of the business process and can even impact employee engagement and performance. For certain companies, IoT in business can help frameworks learn to autonomously execute transactions in supply chains if certain requirements meet.

New and exciting advancements that could make the future of IoT extremely versatile. Some of them include battery-free sensors, a wide range of wearable innovations, as well as "minuscule" AI microcontrollers. Additionally, there are numerous organization changes occurring in the work to improve the appearance of IoT devices. As an example, network cutting could be used to provide lower-dormancy, higher-speed data transfer relationships for greater reliability for strategic devices.

Participate in IoT by embracing advances like artificial reasoning (AI) as well as 5G there are a lot of opportunities for businesses. Urban areas are increasingly managed with IoT and security systems, the system is operating regularly. Massive assembly tasks could link all office machines with remote-checking frameworks. Service companies can gather details from the brilliant meters and the base. Medical equipment can make use of IoT technology to relay the status of a patient to physicians. The ranchers are able to streamline their gathering by using IoT research. IoT is a fantastic tool for many companies.

Thus, IoT will permit organizations to be more able to assist their clients as well as manage their employees and also work on their products, managements and cycle.

How IoT Helped During

In the year 2020, what's going on in IoT? Perhaps the most recent IoT advancements were used to solve the challenges brought on from the pandemic that swept the world:

Highlights of smart building Secure offices are essential to stop any spread of COVID-19 and IoT allowed for control of access to and filter natural characteristics such as particulate matter, and volatile naturally occurring blends (VOCs). Heating, ventilation and air conditioning (HVAC) frameworks could be integrated with IoT to ensure that you have an flexible structure maintenance that conforms to safety procedures.

• Touchless assistance: limiting the actual interaction between employees customers, gadgets, and clients was made possible with the help of IoT. From innovative installment methods to programmatic temperature monitoring and wellness screening on a section, IoT could completely eliminate the necessity for communication.

The following observations: Many office buildings have employed IoT in order to track and monitor the possibility of contamination. It is possible to use sensors to measure the amount of people in a particular part of the building and increase the frequency of sterilization exercises. Additionally, they can monitor the temperature of people who come in to identify potential risk.

In general, IoT and related innovations can be considered a significant advantage in fighting the spread of.

Follow these steps on how to make use of IoT to benefit Your Business

When it comes to the best way to integrate in the Internet of Things in organizations one of the most crucial things to remember is that these technological advancements in communication and interconnectedness can be hugely beneficial to practically every business. The method that every company decides to utilize IoT within its own sector or industry is a crucial choice. This isn't an all-inclusive method, but rather an extremely modified method for getting a better understanding of implementing and upgrading objectives for the business.

To illustrate this, there are couple of key issues or benefits of IoT which a variety of organizations could examine for their individual ideas for developing:

Check out the huge information available: Examining and analyzing vast amounts of information may provide insights of a variety of variables crucial to the efficient operation of any business. In the first place, IoT is of paramount important, IoT can give experiences of extremely important market trends in addition to the way that items are executed. These experiences can be used in order to improve the short and long-term strategies for business.

• Connect each client and client IoT provides the information you need about each particular client so that you can provide personalized administration. Furthermore, with IoT devices that connect you with your client base, you are able to sift through details to be able to see every phase of your customers' purchasing cycle - starting with how they search to the way they shop and make use of your services and products. This allows you to develop more effective and engaging marketing efforts.

Remote labor force Studies show that remote work is growing. Thanks to IoT it is possible for remote labor forces to be more closely connected to everything from documents to equivalent stock with greater utility and a greater range of tasks that could be accomplished from afar.

Increase your visibility from more innovative marketing strategies that keep you connected with your clients, to greater interactions with everyone in your work force IoT lets your business expand its reach both to buyers and reps. In addition, by forming collaboration agreements like Presence that are offered by Consolidated Technologies, Inc. It allows you to achieve the levels of speed and flexibility which make your presence visible as it expands.

Consolidated Technologies, Inc. and the Internet of Things are taking off.

Naturally in the current environment, in the age of IoT and application for business set to expand the scope of your business, you'll need an exchange and IT partner to guide you through all the modern advancements so that you are able to effectively utilize this breakthrough technology and any subsequent data to inform your strategy of actions. It is for this reason that you require Consolidated Technologies, Inc. to make plans for the future of your enterprise. We do not just offer technology solutions - we understand your challenges to communicate the latest technology!

WAYS THE INTERNET OF THINGS (IOT) CAN ASSIST WITH DEVELOPING YOUR BUSINESS

Today, we live in an age of technological technology where everyone on the planet is connected by the use of some gadgets that connect to the internet. The collection of devices which are connected to us is referred to as"The Internet of Things (IoT). The IoT gadgets include all types of technological devices that can be connected through the World Wide Web. Most likely the most prominent IoT devices you'll see in your house include video reconnaissance security systems.

If you're determined to be successful, regardless of whether you're a startup or one with a history of decades, it is essential to make use of every single one of the options available as well as your competition are going to leave if that they use IoT to their specific businesses. Whatever your firm's situation, even if it does not have an E-trade strategy it is essential to know about IoT and determine ways to incorporate with your organization in order to get the most effective results required to create and outperform in the competition. The most essential equipment to use in IoT is to establish an effective web connection. Of the many renowned ISPs that are available, Spectrum assumes control with comprehensive Spectrum software that can provide you with amazing speeds and limit limits for similar circumstances.

This is part of ways of how IoT will assist you in growing your company.

1. The Stock Administration

Many businesses need at least a few items of it, regardless if they own stores or a distribution center stuffed with things. Handling stocks is an essential task that can determine how successful. Instead of depending on multiple people to manage the stock, it's possible to use a computer with programs to track sources that are entering or out of stocks. This way of managing stock will reduce the risk of items being lost in transporting them or moving them. ERP software can be extremely helpful in directing inventory.

2. Checking Performance and Security

IoT will simply monitor stock and assist in reviewing the appearance of employees as they're moving items. IoT helps companies with improving their execution by examining the quality of their work and ensuring that it is done so. Monitoring hardware with video monitoring can help in protecting your workplace from theft. Remote security tools can be put in place to ensure that the authorities are aware suspicious behavior as quickly as they can and are able to be quick to respond.

3. Sharing of information

The data gathered through inventory administration and performing checks can then be shared with the relevant people using IoT. Information can be distributed to remote locations. The distribution centre, located miles from your workplace. If your company requires to handle global clients, they could get information to them within a few minutes.

4. Continuous Analytics

Sharing information can happen in real-time. In-continuous Analytics could aid in increasing the efficiency of your work when individuals can access information readily and in a gradual manner. Therefore, rather than waiting longer for data to reach them, they will be able to tackle the project quickly and effectively. With Real-Time

5. Computerized Marketing

The computerized marketing system is an important showcase device your business must have. Advertising is the best way to get your product in the hands of buyers. Your promotions can be tailored to the target audience you want. Through the use of digital showcasing tools, such as Google Ads Your advertisement will then be shown at the right time to your targeted audience. Virtual Entertainment is a fantastic method of connecting

6. Omni-channel approach

A multichannel method of dealing discounts benefits both the customer as well as the retailer or maker. The ability to send all correspondence in one place helps build trust, and also avoids make a mistake between two parties. In fact, within the company, this method helps the smuggling of data and allows every piece of information and data being able to get across to everyone in the company by using ERP software.

7. The executive's competence

The various methods that we have discussed all share the same thing to all intents and purposes. It is efficiency. The ability to produce is essential for the growth of a company. It can help companies cut down on costs and also buyers by obtaining the best product due to this. The success of a business that is efficient can be considered to be progress.

8. Watching out for Customer Demands

IoT will gather data on current fashions and needs within the purchasing area which means that the company will be able to respond to the needs. Businesses can create products by preparing them according to the needs determined by the expected requests from observing the conduct of shoppers within their business. Companies can collect data about which kind of merchandise is more popular and gain advantages by utilizing IoT applications.

9. Further developing Customer Experience

IoT can help both the company and its customers. Customer feedback is a fantastic technique for improving the client satisfaction, and an online presence for entertainment can help with this. Inviting your customers into conversations and keeping tabs at their needs will enhance the customer experience and help them return to the business to purchase their next product.

BUSINESS EFFECTIVENESS OF THE INTERNET OF THINGS (IOT)

IoT also known as the web of Things is a system of devices and vehicles, machines as well as other items that are fitted with sensors, hardware networks, programming and actuators. They are able to communicate and exchange data. The simplest way to describe it is that IoT gadgets exchange information within the form of a remote or wired organization.

The above definition has the potential for a wide range of outcomes which IoT technologies can provide to our world, changing it from the ground up. The impact of IoT is most evident in business because it has, not only has it altered the methods used to accomplish various work processes, but also it also changed the way the data is processed and exchanged.

The world of business is evolving due to the introduction of IoT and the associated ways.

Stock Tracking and Management

Do you rely on warehouse capacity and storage? Are you faced with issues related to stock-following and management? Do you have your team too caught up on settling matters relating to stocks? Your best chance to changes is right now! IoT innovations can aid you to monitor and follow stocks by offering you the ability to make decisions that are naturally controlled. You heard it correctly! IoT technology and devices are a possibility to introduce them into your capacity units as well as distribution centers that can aid to monitor stock fluctuations as your staff members can focus in a more focused manner on more intellectually demanding projects.

Information Sharing And Perception

Every organization works and grows through the use of data trading and assortment The introduction of IoT is revolutionizing the manner in which information is handled. In addition to providing greater access to customer information, IoT gadgets track and document the ways in which customers interact with devices. These gadgets are smarter, which allows they to deliver a more satisfying customer experience while at the while helping companies understand this information to aid in growth and improvement. The information is used by organizations to determine the customer cycles, customer requirements as well as the development level in addition to creative concepts in the form of strategies to publicize and marketing. The data can be collected or shared with others, then decoded using IoT technological innovation.

Usefulness And Efficiency

With more information on markets and customers The value of any company can increase dramatically. IoT devices can be linked with each other and monitored for further improvement that in turn enhances how effective the company is. It is possible to do more faster. IoT software and devices allow employees to accomplish huge projects in a speedier and error-free style. A boost in effectiveness and efficiency will increase your advantages significantly. It is merely a matter of ensuring the equipment you use is of high-quality and that it is maintained regularly to avoid negative effects on efficiency and effectiveness.

Remote Work

Thanks to IoT technology, you do not require to be there in order to perform your tasks. If the business you work for doesn't have to handle actual inventory, then it is the time to you could make use of IoT technology since it allows the employees to communicate with each other and work remotely research has proven that people who telecommute are happier and efficient that will significantly enhance your company's capabilities.

Gifted Workers

The fact that IoT devices and programs require crucial information as well as the ability to cooperate in the field of innovation is a requirement that businesses focus on a team of experts capable of handling IoT innovations successfully. Hiring someone who can only marginally benefit from IoT innovations won't let them spend time and money but additionally, it will negatively influence the efficiency of the enterprise. If businesses begin to hire these individuals, they are likely to lean towards modern technology and this will also increase their motivation for undertakings in the future.

IoT advancements have created the concept of smart homes possible, and currently an opportunity to create amazing work environments has been uncovered. Companies that accept this change are likely to see an increase in their development rates as opposed to those that remain skeptical regarding this idea. Be aware of where you are and then make your selection in the same the same way.

IN WHAT WAYS WILL THE INTERNET OF THINGS AFFECT THE WAY WE WORK?

"The "Web of Things" (IoT) might seem to be an advanced wave of talk coolers, self-starting cars and even robots, but Internet-connected devices that communicate together will affect our daily lives outside of our "savvy home," too. for workers, IoT will significantly have an impact on the way of working in terms of saving time and resources and opening doors for growth and improvement.

1. A lot more details

The Internet of Things will be an information device. It is a sign that companies must examine how they collect and analyze data. Not solely will they have to adapt and learn new types of data insights however, the amount and variety of data generated through IoT can also create opportunities for tacticians, information specialists and even customer support.

"Organizations will approach a gigantic surge of information that this large number of associated gadgets will produce," stated Mary J. Cronin, an instructor of Boston College, Carroll School of Management and the creator of "Brilliant Products, Smarter Services: Strategies for Embedded Control." "Yet that information should be broken down to see more about clients and patterns. Organizations should begin involving IoT information as a component of their preparation to remain cutthroat and to offer creative new administrations and items."

2. Find out where everything is continuously

"IoT can possibly make the work environment life and business processes significantly more useful and proficient," Cronin declared.

A major method IoT improves usability and increase productivity is by creating a system that makes area follow-up quicker and easier. IoT-connected devices and equipment are expected to be branded geologically everywhere, similar to what has been done already at emergency facilities, thereby which will save laborers the time of searching for things down, and also saving money as well by reducing the risk of accidents.

"Organizations may track every aspect of their business, from managing inventory and responding to requests as quickly as possible to locating and dispatching field administration personnel. Devices and manufacturing plants and vehicles will be generally associated and detailing their areas," Cronin explained.

3. Go anyplace quicker

IoT is the next big feature of the daily commute. Connectivity of mobile cellphones, cars, as well as the road you travel to will aid in reducing the time spent traveling, which will allow people to go to more quickly or get work completed in record time.

In the present, the "associated vehicle" is only the start of IoT capabilities. "AT&T, along with automakers like GM and BMW, are adding LTE network to the vehicle and making new associated administrations, like ongoing traffic data and continuous diagnostics for the front seat and infotainment for those in the rearward sitting arrangement," stated Macario Namie, vice president of advertising for Jasper Wireless, a machine-to-machine (M2M) stage manufacturer.

Then, IoT will incorporate everything from stoplights to roads.

"Envision a world in which a city's framework introduced a side of the road sensors, whose information could be utilized to examine traffic designs around the city and change traffic signal tasks to limit or maybe wipe out gridlocks," Namie explained. "This could save a couple of moments, in the event that not hours of our day."

4. Less expensive, greener assembling

Due to IoT connectivity to gadgets, interconnectivity between devices can be a result of the reception from "shrewd matrix" innovations, that make use of sensors, meters and various other gadgets to monitor the progress of energy. It can also include elective sources of force such as the sun-based or wind.

"The Internet of Things will definitely bring down costs in the assembling industry by lessening wastage, utilization of fuel, and the disposing of financially unviable resources," Namie stated. "IoT can likewise work on the productivity of energy creation and transmission and can additionally decrease discharges by working with the change to renewables."

5. The cell phones are completely off the grid and the top high-level executives (MDM)

IT divisions could be granted remote access to computers and cellphones. But, IoT will likewise empower control of devices that are connected to the internet according to Roy Bachar, organizer and the CEO MNH

Innovations. MNH Innovations and an individual of the Internet of Things Council.

Bachar who is also involved as a consultant for CommuniTake the company which offers remote access technology, stated the most advanced technology available gives them complete control over tablets and cell phones is currently allowing remote administration of various devices, such as Android cameras, set-top boxes and even TVs as well as other devices.

Soon, MDM innovations will reach into the distant management of IoT devices, and can bring changes to IT departments and IoT-related representatives.

"Obviously, the media transmission goliaths will assume a significant part in the IoT area, and they are on the whole presenting arrangements. I trust that as of mid-2014, we will see the presentation of stages for dealing with the IoT applications as well as arrangements presented by organizations, like communicate, for far off administration of IoT gadgets," Bachar explained.

6. Intricacy of the board

According to Bachar As the number of devices that they are connected to grows and the complexity of managing these devices. Today, for instance the workforce uses mobile phones to keep in touch, improve efficiency, and distraction. In the future, with IoT phones, they'll be able to perform additional functions, such as control of IoT-related devices. "A significant number of things to come IoT-associated gadgets won't have a screen. The method for assuming command of the gadget will be by means of cell phones," Bachar explained.

"The intricacy will likewise build because of the assortment of working frameworks," Bachar said. Therefore, IT representatives and offices will have an diverse range of platforms to oversee, not only Android as well as iOS, Bachar said.

These two scenarios may need preparation for employees to determine how they can manage and supervise the associated devices that cross-stage.

7. You will be able to cut down on time and enjoy more of your work day when you have a plan in advance.

Apart from managing the other IoT devices, your mobile phone could also function to a controller in your everyday life, claimed Brendan Richardson, prime supporter and the CEO of PsiKick which is a Charlottesville, Va.- founded startup which develops IoT remote sensor.

One of the greatest advantages of IoT is that it gives you devices which "know" you and will aid in saving time, allowing you to move in and out of places and handle exchanges faster using the cell phone.

"The iPhone or Android will progressively communicate with an entire scope of sensors that you never see and don't possess, yet which furnish your cell phone with significant data and follow up for your sake through an application," Richardson explained.

These sensors will ensure that having your coffee in the morning can eliminate the necessity of waiting to wait in line, ensuring an easier start to your day. Remote sensors, for instance, detect when you walk through an Starbucks that alerts the barista about your possible need based on your previous requests. The barista can either affirm your request or choose an alternative request to pay for it by phone Richardson explained.

8. There is a good chance that you will have to be more productive

IoT could make workers' lives simpler on several aspects, however Richardson declared that IoT can also bring about massive shifts for every sector.

"Each business and each industry will be disturbed over the course of the following

30 years," Richardson declared. "We're seeing this presently starting with the ordinary Internet. It's being driven by information and huge scope efficiencies when you convert something to bits as opposed to iotas."

Richardson spoke of the growth of rental films, for instance.

"Netflix pretty much obliterated Blockbuster by utilizing the Internet to immeasurably work on the planned operations of trading DVDs and eliminating annoying late charges. Then, at that point, they changed over the particles of a DVD into bits and conveyed 80% of their films over broadband at this point. [You get] more films on request and lower costs. Furthermore, a whole industry - the DVD rental business - is committed to the chronicle of history."

Richardson claimed that disturbances like this will be common in all industries therefore, the organizations and their leaders should be prepared.

THE INTERNET OF THINGS (IOT) CAN ASSIST YOUR ECOMMERCE EFFORT IN MANY WAYS

The emergence of Internet of Things (IoT) devices has brought with it an unpredictably shift in internet-based marketplace as shoppers' lifestyles continue to change and evolving to become more flexible.

In addition, the rapid amount of customers who are embracing the internet has witnessed online business grow continuously and will become the future of the retail industry as the major portion of this growth takes place in the technological market.

The year 2016 was the most successful, and according to Statista the global deals in eCommerce retail were reported at an astounding $1.85 trillion. They are expected in 2021 to be $4.88 trillion.

Retailers are also getting ready to take on their customers' needs with the Internet of Things in a attempt to improve the experiences of buyers around the globe. It is clear that both the web-based as well as retail sectors must maintain a steady pace over trends of the modern advertising world for them to be successful and serious.

However what exactly can a business that is online poised to gain enormously by benefiting from IoT? What kind of changes are taking place today and how will they affect the business of online? Are internet-based businesses able to have an impact on their work and attract potential customers?

Instructions to Use the Internet of Things to Grow Your Ecommerce Business

These are some of the most exciting ways online-based companies can profit through IoT.

1. Strategies and better following

Through IoT the retailers gain notable permeability in the process of customer satisfaction so that they are able to meet the demands of buyers who buy online more often.

IoT technology offers online business retailers the opportunity to follow clients' orders right from the time they are placed until the next time delivery to the customer's doorstep.

Retailers now have the ability to track every item of inventory by way of board-based frameworks so that they are able to find their merchandise, paying no attention to where they're.

Cloud-based innovations including GPS or RFID (Radio Frequency Identification) likewise give retailers data on the status of traffic, weather locations, areas and even professors, which makes efficient operations for the managers more competent.

The system also automates transport and transportation to stop the problem that result from lost or damaged shipments, while also improving the vehicle's training.

2. Stock management using computers

Online business stores have the advantage of having control over items that are going out and coming out of their stores to see what's available and what is not.

With such a wide array of tools as IoT sensors and RFID tags included in stock frameworks the business process can become easier. Furthermore, retailers should not involve head supervisors in order to truly check inventory as they are able to keep track of their inventory.

In this way, IoT benefits internet business by allowing it to gather and transfer pertinent and updated information on items to ERP frameworks.

It additionally lessens human blunder in stock-taking and requesting/reordering of things.

Furthermore, with brilliant racks and temperature-observing sensors, retailers would follow be able to stock, yet in addition, check ideal temperatures for things that are transient and get moment alarms when they're required.

Stock administration using iot

3. Connects are improved between makers and consumers at the end

IoT ensures that a good relationship is outlined via the connected devices in a manner that both clients and the maker of the product are in a relationship that is drawn out.

For example, the makers of printers may supply cartridges that are different from original printers.

So, the name is in the minds of buyers throughout the life of the item.

In addition, IoT can give new revenue streams for retailers through developing new programs of action including contributing to the continuous management such as prescient support remote monitoring, remote check-ins, and testing for the specific item.

4. Individualized information and actions

IoT is also an opportunity to combine personal data with that of companies for more tailored experiences.

As a result, internet-based retail stores can benefit from buyer's association to give specific information and actions and combining information to personalize the experience for families, and to each part of.

A real model will be one where there is a vehicle that's associated with it that the driver is able to receive offers that are tailored to his/her. However families with excellent refrigerator could get meals tailored to the preferences of their family.

When advanced marketers gain details and understand buyer behavior, they are able to use it to reach out to their customers, and affect their purchasing decisions on customer's business.

5. Internet-connected business websites that are IoT-associated

The online shopping trend has grown, and with it comes a need for sellers to ensure that the customer satisfaction is as simple as possible.

In the age of IoT the need for retailers to find a way to make use of the data coming in from various sources and devices, while being sensitive, and not only to devices such as iPads or phones but also to other articles to other items.

As a result, retail stores could create websites with responsiveness which make the most of IoT to improve the user experience when browsing the internet.

6. Processes for shopping that are automated

Thanks to IoT the possibility of mechanized checkouts is becoming a possibility as is the case with Amazon Go. Amazon Go is presenting.

It means that the buying system will be automated, and customers arrive, make purchases then leave and are charged for the purchase on their mobile phones.

Additionally, in the future advanced frameworks will recognize the moment when customers are ready to go for shopping, and they will have their bags ready for them according to their purchase record.

In the event that they give them the details of what they'll need to purchase to the candy machines, all they need to can do is based on the drive-through. They're completely set.

Ways IoT Is Reinventing Businesses Today

The Internet of Things (IoT) involves more than simply connecting devices and systems. It's opening amazing opportunities to create the most innovative services and products that weren't before thought possible. In a recent Forbes Insights survey of 700 CEOs, 60% of companies are either creating or transforming with new business lines through their IoT initiatives. Meanwhile, 36 percent are pondering the possibility of innovative business models. Additionally, 63% of companies have, at present providing new or updated benefits to their customers directly due to their IoT capabilities.

Making use of IoT is a result of an availability method as a change process for businesses and has proven results, with the added benefit of increased profits. Seven out of 10 executives accept IoT as a way to increase revenue. At present, 45 percent of them say IoT can help support the benefits of 1% up to 5%. further 41% claim that the impact has benefited them increase their earnings by 5 to 15 per year. The coming year will basically all of them of them, 94%, anticipate an increase in benefits of not lower than 5% or 15% due to IoT.

But, the benefits of IoT extend beyond the benefits of generating income. Here are five alternative methods IoT will impact businesses in the present.

Chapter 4: First Let Us Agree That The Internet Of Things Is Not A Hype

We have to admit it: there are numerous technological advancements happening right now, and we're not deficient of hype-words.

In the past, it was known as the Cloud while last year was big data, and this year, it appears like the Internet of Things. In the midst of all the buzz, it is important to know if these technologies are actually revolutionary or just the noise. Let's look at the facts.

When we were our Neanderthal ancestors likely there was plenty of buzz around too. A new spear design, or modern flint stone designs (not the ones in cartoons) or arrowheads would have caused a stir. The idea was passed on through the centuries and perhaps just a few thousand years ago generated excitement over things such as the creation of irrigation systems, wheels and the like. Around a hundred years ago the pace of innovation accelerated into technology and warfare, like improved weapon designs and the development of gunpowder, and perhaps more effective methods to detect the presence of disease.

Now, we are in 2016, and the internet isn't a novelty to the contemporary world, but there are substantial parts of the globe and an overwhelming majority of the people who do not have internet access.

What makes the internet remarkable is the amount of creativity it has set off through the development of an environment powered by technology. That's the internet is the perfect example. My 14 year old nephew doesn't understand what the world without internet could be like. IoT or the Internet of Things or IoT is one such thing that have been made via the internet. Technology is constantly evolving, as do the other areas which are powered by the internet. Moore's law states that the speed of technology is expected to double in two years. However, we're seeing this law breaking due to a faster growth of technology. There is no reason to be surprised therefore that a new technology such as"the internet of things" might possess the potential to be an extremely fast-growing technology, in the event that this is what we're trying to create initially.

UNDERSTANDING WHAT IOT REALLY IS?

IoT is the short version of Internet of Things. It's the name given to the technology which allows IP sensor devices to accomplish a particular job of measuring an sensor and possibly responding to input or create an answer through various linked systems. The other terms, such as Internet of Everything (IoE), Internet of Devices (IoD) and others are variations on the primary word IoT.

Here's an illustration. A IoT powered device, coupled to internet somehow, skateboard is able to measure distances the rider has traveled. It could relay this information to an application that is gathering the data, for instance using a smartphone with an application developed by the maker of the skateboards to accomplish this exact reason. Now we can are able to use an Internet skateboard that is connected to the Internet.

In a higher and higher level, and based on a more advanced technological development, think about the skateboard's wheels contain two elements. Sensors that are capable of measuring distance as well as time, and motor-powered wheels that can send a signal via a brain's central nerve to the skateboard, which in turn is connected to a mobile phone and controlled via remote. Now we have a skateboard which can be controlled, and give us additional details on which to make our choices about the best way to use it. This is what we call The Internet of Things.

Make this available to all devices or application, and let your brain be awestruck.

It is now possible to talk about an array of topics that range from Diapers to Spaceships. The objects and devices will grow smart and connected to the Internet, transferring hundreds of gigabytes worth of data daily, or perhaps every minute. Think about this. A single Boeing 787 flight creates around fifty percent of an Terrabyte of data. And this is despite the fact that there's not a significant increase in IoT devices in a typical air carrier in the present. Imagine the possibility of an airline equipped with a variety of IoT equipment that makes the customer experience entirely different to that which is currently. It will change everything. From the airline flying high-speed and efficient plane to customers who have an experience unlike anything before, and then in the middle the data analysts, technicians, decision makers, and other people with the responsibility to analyse all of the information collected by each IoT sensor in the aircraft as well as ensuring better results across all aspects such as passenger satisfaction or flight schedule optimization improving fuel efficiency, and more.

HOW DO WE AS TECHNOLOGISTS EVALUATE TECHNOLOGY ITSELF?

It is the most straightforward explanation. The extent of the possibilities that IoT could accomplish or assist us to accomplish is what makes it so massive as it appears to be. Could this mean that IoT might be more powerful than the development of electricity or, for instance, the wheel? In that case, depending on how we view it, then yes however differently. Let me explain.

The impact of something may be measured by using a number of indicators. The most important thing to consider is how extensive and extensive the consequences can be. Consider the case of climate changes. Changes in the climate is likely to affect the entire range of geographic zones, or even the entire globe. Was there any innovation other than the bulb that is electric? In a world that relied using kerosene and coal bulbs, the development of an illuminated object which was clean and energy efficient was groundbreaking. It was even more revolutionary to be able to expand through the ability to carry energy to distant locations with an electrical wire.

Last example. Penicillin. A world in the grip of large mortality rates due to smallpox and other diseases, Penicillin was an most urgent need that would save not only thousands, but millions of lives. With this in mind, the creation of ketchup seemed to be not a significant event for the majority of people (although Ketchup fanatics may share an opinion).

Chapter 5: How Does Iot Fit Into Our World?

The Internet of Things is a distinct technology framework. It's powered by Internet however it is not an entirely software-driven technology. IoT can be applied to multiple areas of usage and interaction. On one hand, it is fuelled through programming language, codes as well as software in general, but at a different level the IoT manifests itself in physical devices that act according to a specific way, in accordance with what the codes, programming languages and software expect for them to perform.

IOT CAN POTENTIALLY TRANSFORM EVERYTHING

The Internet of Things presents the chance to make the world better. Going deeper into technology may be an enormous leap in comparison to the times when the advent of internet technology was thought as a major move in the right direction. The Internet of

Things will do something that was not done before in a completely new way. More than 50 billion devices are that are expected to be connected to the internet in 2020, the leading experts have reached just the beginning of the Iceberg. What will follow in 2020 will be an enormous increase in the use of IoT devices in our daily and professional life. It is likely that everything will be linked to the internet in some manner and, as the rules for commercializing technology are concerned it is likely that we will be looking to see a massive growth of IoT. IoT driven world. While new businesses and manufactures seek to make money from the more successful and larger gadgets that are being powered and linked with the Internet, small businesses will probably also experience more growth.

The Internet of Things is also closely linked to being the Internet of Everything. There are many more which you've heard, like

Internet of Objects and so on. These are all terms used to describe the same technology, however they are defined differently.

When all is said and done which are the ways to benefit from IoT?

IoT devices, as such, are classified into a variety of categories which can help solve problems or can help to a variety of areas. We will examine a few of them.

LET'S TALK ABOUT SOME SPECIFIC IOT APPLICATIONS

Lynda is undergoing an operation to bypass her. Her physician has instructed that she take a full sleeping in order to recuperate. Lynda issue is that she lives on her own and could not be able to manage taking the care she demands. What would IoT provide any assistance for her If those devices were available? Maybe. If we live in an IoT world that is perfect, Lynda would have access some things that could ease her burden.

For starters, the clothes, they will be connected to IoT to be constantly keeping track of her body temperature as well as changing the comfort level via cooling or warming. It is possible that she sleeps in an IoT mattress that measures whether she's sleeping well and determine if her sleeping pattern is good. It could also be been designed to alter the cushioning depending upon Lynda requires the comfort of a soft bed while she recuperates. Room temperature and lighting will also be controlled by IoT to ensure the proper temperatures, humidity and sufficient lighting when necessary. The kitchen Lynda refrigerator will know the contents and also what Lynda has run out of. The refrigerator can deliver groceries to the home or even healthy meals depending on what she likes.

The doctor who treated Lynda might be able to talk with her and keep track of her progress using a specific device that includes advanced diagnostic features specifically for patients undergoing heart surgery. Medical staff are capable of monitoring her vitals as well as monitor her via remote whenever they wish and for as long as they need to.

Every device has one thing they all have in common. The idea behind"it" being the Internet of Things. The idea is that everyday objects are connected with the internet and be used to accomplish an action, or to automate something which can improve. This opens up the possibility to better connectivity, continuous monitoring, and an action as well as an immediate reaction. The use of IoT can go beyond the ability to connect to devices and let it take action. It is the Internet of Things is about making value out of the devices driven by sensors that can measure the variables and utilize the information to make an informed choice, and possibly send back the command to the device to respond by.

WHAT KIND OF DEVICES CAN CONNECT THROUGH IOT ?

The Internet of Things is not to be mistaken for a remote control toy. The implications and the applications are too complicated.

Industries like Healthcare are able to see an immediate influence from IoT-powered technology however, so too are infrastructure designers using smart cities, agriculture industries, fashion, beverages and food industries as well as services. The applications of IoT within each of these areas according to me, are categorized into two types.

1. The obvious The obvious - These are the applications that can be considered generic, and could not be incredibly specialized. For instance, the IoT powered dishwasher or vacuum cleaner, or Refrigerator. Each of these gadgets is capable of performing certain tasks but they could be restricted to their applications in a wide method.

Cleaners for vacuums clean floors but not make orders for grocery items. Dishwashers clean dishes, but and not even open the door to the kitchen etc.

2. The Unexpected - These gadgets will likely to be very specific regarding their functions and features. Examples that could be used are the human-like robot which can help you arrange your refrigerator, clean your floors and then answer to the door when it is ringing. It could also be the use of nano-robot that could be implanted in the body of the companion we mentioned in the past, Jane. The Nano robots might be able to navigate the blood vessels in her body and relay back data about her disease or damage, as well as items that require repair. Medical professionals, in contrast might be able transmit repair instructions for repair to Nano robots to ensure that they could carry out micro-surgical procedures or even take samples of biopsy to analyze. While

this may be a long way off towards development may be possible.

Chapter 6: How Does The Internet Of Things Benefit Consumers?

For consumers, the only thing you have to just relax and watch for the myriad of internet-connected gadgets to come your way. Sure, the electronic stores will be having the ball. Because mass-produced IoT devices are useful and popular, it's an inevitable conclusion that as the business expands, as does the standard of products and the distinctiveness of the devices hitting the marketplaces. The expectations customers should be able to meet include IoT devices that help them perform things better and more effectively as well as monitoring and measuring devices as well as changes and aiding in gaining more value out of all the things that we carry out in our everyday life. The concept of cars being able to connect with one another is popular and is directly related to IoT for the automotive industry. Healthcare industry IoT could help improve diagnosis, better patient care and improved communication between healthcare professionals and their patients. At schools, IoT devices could help provide the best educational experience to students, and at home, it could help to make your home more efficient secure, comfy and comfortable. There is no limit to what you can do with IoT devices.

DO BUSINESSES HAVE A BENEFIT FROM INTERNET OF THINGS?

What ever industry that you're within, you will be affected through IoT gadgets. Logistics, Energy, Consumer Goods, Healthcare You Name it and you'll find apps (many including today) which connect to the internet and are able to perform a variety of roles. One of the best tips for business owners is to keep an eye on the evolving landscape of business and use technology in order to provide more value your clients. It is also possible to get involved with the IoT industry by creating innovative devices that fulfill an objective and address problems. IoT is currently being utilized in various industries, such as Oil & Gas to monitor pipelines for oil, as well as Smart meters, which aid in measuring and optimizing the supply and consumption of electric power, and in Mining to track the flow of materials. There are many possibilities and we're just starting to explore the possibilities.

No matter who you are or what you do in the coming years, we will witness a massive growth in the field of technology and in particular, the creation of IoT devices. It is believed that the Internet of Things (IoT) framework, or technology, whatever you want to call it could be considered a more advanced technology than anything we've previously seen. Many also consider it to be more than even the web itself. Although we're still at the beginning of technological advancement and the commercialization of it is evident that there is an emerging trend happening. The pace of innovation is increasing day by day as newer gadgets and concepts being developed that will make IoT practical and useful in a myriad of ways. Take part in this new trend today by being aware on the most recent technology developments, as well as engaging in a meaningful conversations on IoT with your family, friends as well as colleagues and fellow peers. There is no telling what a conversation could result!

TRANSFORMING MANUFACTURING INDUSTRIES WITH THE RIGHT INDUSTRIAL IOT APPROACH

The Internet of Things is slowly expanding its capabilities, allowing it to begin solving issues that could really benefit from it. We'll talk about manufacturing and how this Internet of Things may open the doors that would otherwise be impossible to break and open.

THE NEED FOR INDUSTRIAL IOT IN MANUFACTURING

I enjoy conversations that are specifically. Even though being flexible and having an

10,000 feet view can help but it's the in-depth details of details that make these conversations more fascinating. Manufacturing is among the fundamental pillars that make up a developed and stable economy. The global economic output from manufacturing is estimated to be in excess of Trillion dollars annually. China is the only country that has more than 22 percent of all production capacity. Staggering! It is a staggering fact that the United States follows with over 15% of the world's manufacturing being attributed to it. One of the most important verticals, manufacturing creates economies, and is essentially all of globe. It is also possible to say that manufacturing is the main driver of all other industries since everything created through manufacturing gets used in different industries to create other products. Manufacturing in itself is dependent upon manufacturing in order to function. Is that logical?

Manufacturing will undergo a dramatic change due to IoT over the next few decades. What is the question could be: what ?.The internet of Things as is now known can come in various kinds. We can have Human to Machine as well as Machine to Human. the Machine to Machine, or M2M. Numerous experts believe M2M can be a key factor in helping improve manufacturing procedures and will help to change how the manufacturing industry operates. Below are a few examples of what is taking place right now.

According to PWC Global, 35% of US manufacturers are currently collecting and using data generated by smart sensors to enhance manufacturing/operating processes. However, 34% of respondents believe it's "extremely critical" that US manufacturing firms implement an IoT plan for their business. This is extremely interesting and it makes perfect sense that we now take a consider implementing IoT in manufacturing. These benefits will definitely improve manufacturing processes from beginning until the end. As per SAP, Manufacturing will provide an end-to-end view of all stages of production as well as linking your production with the business process you are using. This is important since the gap between the manufacturing process and the enterprise is an area that requires improvements.

Think about the scenario of a plant that makes an item that is fully automated with IoT. The IoT can improve the production process for widgets through more efficient and responsive control of quality production details, quality control and more, but also by connecting production to demands from business. Production could increase or decrease according to the order that are received at a real-time pace and on. Naturally, this will integrate with other connected software like ERP, and many more. These systems will have to undergo their own process of integrating an IoT-powered manufacturing facility.

INDUSTRIAL IOT TODAY

In various varieties it is in many forms, the Industrial Internet of Things (IoT) is in full swing. With more factories using and installing more connected sensors, autonomic communication between the devices and systems gets more simple. Contrary to what is commonly believed that the Internet of Things will be capable of everything, assume control of everything, we must be a bit more cautious and avoid conflating Artificial Intelligence with IoT. The most popular industrial applications for IoT are Shell Oil, John Deere, Cisco, and my most favorite, a myriad of other.

Chapter 7: What Is Next In The Internet Of Things?

It is clear that the Internet of Things is not something that will go away in the future. Similar to other technologies that held the top spot over the past few decades, Cloud technologies are still an area that is still in the process of developing industry and it is impossible to build a real IoT system without Cloud. Big Data Another Internet-related technology, is rapidly expanding to meet the requirements for humans to analyse enormous amounts of information in the shortest amount of time and gain knowledge that can help make important vital decisions in a variety of situations.

The Internet of Things today is the framework used by companies to initiate an era that could have infinite consequences. Gartner is an industry-leading analysis firm, predicts that by 2020, more than 21 billion devices are connected to the internet.

Are these gadgets as good as the Nano-robots? Not all are, however many could be more complicated more than a basic vacuum cleaner. The uses for these gadgets will include efficiency, productivity, improved medical care, speedier processes, more efficient cities, more enthusiastic viewers, innovative educational models as well as a myriad of other methods. What the future holds for IoT in the next five years isn't difficult to predict, considering the amount of data and data that we can access However, as IoT grows, we'll see the rapid growth of technology as well as applications.

Take a look at Moore's Law in the context of that isn't 100 percent applicable in the present because the pace that technology is made is 5 times more than Moore anticipated, however what is fascinating is that the speed of technology developing is rapidly increasing too. It shouldn't come as surprising if industry analysts could be revised in order to predict that 40 billion or 50 billion devices are internet-connected before 2020.

HOW TO GET INVOLVED IN THE INTERNET OF THINGS

This is the path that leads us further into investing money in research, and finding solutions to the problems that we face all over. There is no shortage of issues. Smaller niche businesses have greater creative capabilities than larger companies, which are confronted with various business issues and problems. There is a need for more innovative concepts and ideas for solving challenges than anyone else. Wearables devices, sensors and wearables growing in use in the market, it is sometimes hard to define a certain technology. For instance, would a device worn by a person be classified as a wearable, or one that is an industrial IoT application in the case of industries, and so on.

There are other issues related to security for the devices and sensors made possible through the Internet of Things. Connecting a sensor is susceptible to getting hacked. Which flight do you plan to take entirely powered by IoT could be hacked in mid flight? What impact would a production facility face if compromised and its IoT devices are not properly programmed? What is the price from this? The above and other issues remain open to debate and are awaiting resolution. What is crucial at the present moment is the real-world uses of IoT and the ways it will assist us in an unimaginable manner.

There will be more to discuss the next occasion. Learn how to make the most of IoT and join in important conversations to help develop an unique view, meet important issues and help improve the quality of life in this environment through technological advancements.

Chapter 8: Evolution Of The Iot

History of the Internet of Things

The idea of an Internet of Things has been in use for some time in the past. It was initially known under various names, such as embedded Internet or pervasive computing. The term "Internet of things' was coined through Kevin Ashton in 1999 when he worked at Procter & Gamble.

Ashton sought to get the attention of senior managers when they were working on the most advanced technology, called RFID. Thus, he dubbed the talk "Internet of Things." While it was initially launched to 1999 in the year 2000, it wasn't it not until the year 2010 when the phrase IoT began to gain momentum.

In 2010, it was reported of Google was storing a huge quantity of information for its Street View features. There was much controversy over the possibility that Google would like to use its Street View functions to search the world as similar to the Internet. Similar to that, China announced that it will take the initiative to make IoT an important strategic element in its development strategies.

Many tech giants as well as research companies such as Gartner have begun to talk about IoT among the most exciting technology trends in the past few years. in 2013, IDC issued a research report which predicted IoT to reach 9 trillion dollars by the year 2020.

It was January of 2014 that the concept IoT was officially introduced to the masses and even consumers, in the year that Google revealed it was planning to buy Nest to the tune of $3.2 billion. That same year there was also it was the time that Consumer Electronics Show (CES) was held in Las Vegas under the theme of IoT (Lueth 2014.).

Internet of Things in the Modern Era

It is not a stretch to state it is true that the Internet of Things (IoT) has a direct impact on our society in possible manner. It's drastically changed our way of life as well as work, travel and manage business. Furthermore, IoT has become the base of transformation in the industry. IoT is playing an essential part for Industry 4.0 and bringing the digital revolution to various sectors and schools, cities as well as the entire society.

One of the main reasons IoT is now a vital element of our society is because it acts as a means of connecting the physical and virtual worlds. Users can connect to digital networks and to the Internet via a range of smartphones, tablets, laptops, computers as well as other electronic devices. Through connecting to the Internet users are able to communicate and exchange data, talk to people across the globe, shop online for items as well as many more functions which people use everyday.

In the last couple of several years IoT changed from a simple concept which consists of a few basic protocols for communication and devices, to an entire field where devices, the latest technological advancements, as well as users can create an entire system of innovation, reuse and the interconnectivity of physical and digital worlds.

Purpose of the IoT

IoT basically allows users to connect devices via the Internet. They, or devices that exchange data with each other and transfer data to other intelligent devices as well as systems. They are typically capable of receiving information (i-scoop, 2018,).

In connecting the physical and virtual worlds by bringing physical and virtual worlds together, the Internet of Things has created an enormous impact on the world. Everyone else is aware about the value of IoT and the numerous applications it offers. It is an effective means for businesses to simplify the connection between a variety of intelligent devices as well as human activities.

IoT platforms link a huge quantity of data from various elements of the physical world on the Internet. It is essential to optimize IoT for companies to guarantee an efficient growth process and the highest level of security. Additionally, the development advanced data analysis tools and computers is feasible thanks to IoT because it generates number of income streams for various types of businesses (Virtual Force, 2016,).

Modern Challenges

The initial issues of IoT were all connected to the network of connected objects The current issues and dangers of IoT are mostly attributed to the network technology, interconnected systems, as well as a myriad of applications that are based on the fundamental layers.

In theory, everything can be interconnected to Internet through the use of appropriate IoT technology. This includes objects that are physical along with living organisms which includes animals as well as humans. Therefore, everything and associated parts of complicated physical objects are able to be identified via the Internet of Things.

There's a broad range of these gadgets. Examples of consumers' IoT devices comprise smart watches and smart homes. In the same way, the enterprise IoT as well as industrial IoT comprises modern heavy machinery that are revolutionizing the industry and creating a new paradigm with the help of Industry 4.0.

Thus, the main question is not about the type of network you could connect, rather the issue is what the reason for connecting an item to a network, as well as what the possibilities of outcomes as well as risks can be. Each item has unique advantages and disadvantages when being connected to the Internet. In general, the process of capturing data as well as transmitting and receiving information are the major objectives of using IoT technology.

IoT Use Cases

Everyone should be aware that IoT is a vast concept that includes a myriad of instances, different techniques, protocols and even applications. Additionally, it integrates with a variety of other technologies such as machine learning and artificial intelligence to achieve the results you want.

The majority of IoT equipment and assets are required been designed with electronic devices including actuators, sensors and various other elements that enable the devices to connect with one another and to capture information, process, and share important information.

The connection of IoT and the use of IoT data can allow different kinds of organizations, consumers as well as industries to make huge improvements and new ideas to their processes. Many industries, including transportation, healthcare and finance are already altered through IoT. The purposes of IoT generally fall into various use cases meaning the main goal of using IoT as well as what the business hopes to accomplish with the use of this technology. Like, for instance, the home automation system and monitoring of assets, health as well as environmental change, among numerous others.

This simply means that there could be thousands and hundreds of IoT applications as they are different from industry sector and also the nature of use. Some IoT applications are common as they can be found in virtually every field. For example, tracking assets is a common application. All industries require consumers to keep track of their belongings as well as cargo companies employ similar technologies to monitor various containers and their orders. A few fundamental distinctions when it comes to the application of the universal IoT applications are present However, the basic features are generally the same.

Chapter 9: What Is The Iot In The Moment?

Internet of Things (IoT) is regarded as an efficient and contemporary concepts that is bringing industry's revolution. It has helped in the development of various other technologies digital too. In the end, IoT has changed the way companies manage business operations.

Many experts believe IoT to be a disruptive force within the tech and business sector. Therefore, businesses must evaluate their needs as well as the potential results before they implement these solutions across all business and in different industries.

Because IoT is an idea that's used in a myriad of multidisciplinary ideas and visions It is evident that the uses of IoT do not limit to a specific area or sector. Indeed, IoT touches all areas of society.

Virtual Personal Assistants and IoT

Virtual Personal Assistants (VPAs) are becoming increasingly well-known, not just in homes, but also in workplaces as well as in various businesses around the globe. VPAs are an integral part of the intelligent technology that can comprehend the required information either in written or spoken form and accomplishing this task once they have understood the request.

An enviable IT service provider, Cognizant, is predicting that the market value of the VPAs market will be around $1 billion in 2024 (Cognizant 2019). The tech giants Google and Apple dominate the virtual assistant market.

Popular VPAs

The majority of people around all over the world The entry point for the IoT is the smart speaker and digital personal assistants. Amazon as well as Google particularly have been leading the way in this field using the latest technology and devices. Voice control is now one of the top users of the market of smart home technology and regulating day-today tasks through your mobile devices.

Here are a few of the most well-known VPAs which are available on the marketplace (Vergara 2020):

Apple's Siri

Siri from Apple Siri is an extremely loved VPA. It's built in the iPhone as of iPhone 4S. In the past, Siri has evolved a quite a bit and has been used on many different Apple gadgets like MacBook, iPad, and other devices. It is able to provide a range of features that can be controlled by voice and also handle various other features such as alarms, web services and weather functions, messages, notes play music, and so on.

Microsoft's Cortana

Microsoft launched its VPA in 2009, and named it Cortana. The VPA is user-friendly that enables Windows users to receive assistance for a myriad of functions, including scheduling appointments, making calendars and alarms, talking to individuals, and swiftly launching many applications and software using Windows laptops and Microsoft mobile phones.

One of the most intriguing features is the fact that it has advanced AI capabilities which allow users to find responses to various queries. Since Cortana is able to handle the tasks of smartphones and laptops It is a huge benefit for people who wish to establish a stable and efficient VPA to use for use in business.

Google Assistant

Google Assistant is one of the most well-known and sophisticated VPAs present on the market. It is compatible with various systems including Android platforms as well as Google Smart Home. The company has succeeded in making itself an established name in the market due to the fact that Google continually releases new updates to give a wide range of capabilities that will meet the demands of many users.

Furthermore, Google Assistant is an outstanding example of why VPAs can be considered IoT instruments since they can connect multiple devices to the internet. The users just need to speak into the Assistant via writing it, or by speaking into this extremely efficient device. Google promises that it will improve it possible to make the Assistant more natural it can be in order for users to be able to have a comfortable two-way dialogue using it. The type of voice character can be extremely useful in customer service system as well.

Amazon Alexa

Amazon Alexa is also a well-known brand in the VPA business. It's mainly used in Alexa, which is the Amazon Echo. Alexa's feature Alexa is quite similar to the other VPAs. One of Alexa's distinct benefits is the fact that it permits users to instantly connect their Prime accounts with Alexa. Simply put, customers can purchase and streaming music on Amazon Music, Pandora, or Spotify via Alexa.

Samsung's Bixby

Samsung launched Bixby in the year 2017. As compared to the VPAs from top technology companies, Bixby is an older VPA that is quite distinct from other. Bixby functions as an app that lets you manage the settings of your phone using specific terms or utilize the algorithms within the Home function to find recommendations on the Internet in relation to your activities as well as the items you may have looked up before.

Working of VPAs

There are many VPAs that are available which differ in many ways. But the basic basis of all these VPAs will be identical. VPAs employ passive listening in response to requests or messages like "Hey Siri.' Active listening implies that your device will always be aware of the events going on in the surrounding area. This means that there's a few privacy issues related to VPAs also.

VPAs require connectivity to the Internet for the necessary tasks, such as conducting internet searches, or connecting to other devices. As the virtual assistants that are in your phones are passive devices usually require an activation signal from a wake-up call.

However, it's likely that the device will record without any specific alarm. In the past, for instance, months ago, Amazon Echo has recorded the sounds of murder and has highlighted that certain VPAs can record constantly.

If you speak to your VPA via your mobile phone's speaking, you're basically asking Siri to execute the action you instruction. If, for instance, you ask "Hey Siri Pick an amount between one and 100. This Assistant's virtual Assistant will then select random numbers. If it's not able to comprehend your commands then it will notify you that.

This is a list of common problems which VPAs could not provide an response immediately, and may not understand your question. In these instances it is necessary to communicate clearer, less or faster, or be required to revise the query. In certain instances it is necessary communicate with your VPA repeatedly. In the case of, for instance, when you make a call to an Uber You will be required be able to provide more information, such as the current location of your phone and the your destination in order to make a reservation for the ride.

With smartphones, the user can quickly activate their personal assistants. To activate Siri as well as Google Assistant, the users must hold the home button of the device until they are able to type in the commands or talk into the speaker once it announces "listening.' In contrast smart speakers, such as Amazon Echo are capable of responding only to commands made by voice.

Current Trends of VPAs

The majority of researches and forecasts about VPAs proved to be very accurate as they have been a booming industry into 2020. In addition, lots of individuals companies, industries, and businesses use VPAs for the purpose of enhancing their operations and reap numerous advantages of this technologies.

These days, VPAs aren't just limited to certain industries or users. Large organizations as well as multinational corporations are also using VPAs in order to more effectively manage massive amounts of data they collect and to use the latest analytical tools to increase the quality of their customer service. Many businesses utilize VPAs for everyday tasks, such as the prioritization of appointments and emails simpler and efficient for the staff and customers.

In the end, virtual personal assistants have a significant impact on various industries such as IT manufacturing, healthcare, as well as finance. This kind of technology can create a variety of options for a wide range of places. As an example banks are cutting down on the size of their branches with fronts. Instead, huge virtual banking networks are being created to assist clients by providing virtual assistants that improve the efficiency of their systems and their overall effectiveness.

Evolution of IoT During the COVID-19 Pandemic

In the year 2019 2019, it was estimated that the Internet of Things industry worth approximately $150 billion. The amount will grow up to $243 billion by 2021. The main reason behind this substantial increase is due to the outbreak of coronavirus which has provided a massive growth to the IoT sector. Remote working, speedy video conference and transmission chain tracking contactsless payment, and the overall the concept of Industry 4.0 are all possible because of many IoT applications. Before the outbreak IoT technologies, some of the IoT techniques that were commonly utilized by different companies were sensors (85 percent) as well as processing of data (78 percent) and cloud computing technology (75 75 percent) (Infraspeak in 2020).

Here are a few of the most popular apps of IoT which have proved useful at this time of change:

Smart Sensors

Ventilation for different kinds of structures has been a big problem for various architects and developers. Commercial structures, in particular, are more susceptible to pollution of the air that circulates due to the high levels of dust, carbon monoxide and trace levels of pesticides. Although there have been such concerns for many years managing these issues has become more crucial more than ever. It is crucial to install a well-designed ventilation system that can ensure that there is no contamination by the coronavirus and to ensure the highest level of safety.

In these situations Smart sensors can play an important function. Smart sensors are a fantastic use of IoT. They have the capability of determining the air quality at a moment's notice and help to prevent transmission of diseases and polluting. Although these sensors aren't able to detect the virus that causes SARS-CoV-2 through the atmosphere, their uses increase as the monitoring of the quality of air has taken on an immense importance.

The owners of numerous businesses building, structures, and particularly commercial malls are taking advantage of the benefits of intelligent sensors as they're among the most efficient and most affordable solutions on the market, that can collect data on air quality. Furthermore, the sensors work with powerful AI systems that are able to activate and shut down the heating, ventilation and air conditioning (HVAC) systems as required.

Robots

Research and development is taking place within the automation and robotics business for some time until. In the wake of COVID-19 and the strict guidelines for social distancing as well as the supply chain an assembly line that connects many companies have experienced a lot of disruption. With this kind of situation factories must rethink their models of business to comply with the requirements of their customers without jeopardizing current safety standards. This means that numerous companies must rely on IoT to succeed in high-risk industries and streamline the business operations.

Contrary to popular belief The purpose of robots isn't replacing workers instead, they are designed to make procedures more productive, efficient as well as safer. Smart robots' applications are limitless. They are able to transport different types of materials, equipment or even food items. Certain restaurants have made announcements about measures such as the use of drones for delivery, contactless dining or making use of robots to deliver food. In addition, hospitals have also taken these measures since robots are able to quickly connect to other people, without worry of contamination.

Healthcare

IoT has assisted in helping the industry of healthcare to grow across a variety of ways.

Technologies have been a major factor in the improvement of healthcare and medical services. Today, technologies like interactive medicine and telemedicine are possible only because of IoT technology.

A variety of technologies used to Industry 4.0 have applications in the health industry too. As an example, IoT allows experts to connect radiology and imaging equipment. In the same way, it's now easy to monitor remotely patients using the instruments and techniques that are available to Telemedicine. Robotics' use in surgery are also growing quickly as robots can provide a degree of precision difficult to reach with the hand of a human.

A few countries such as Italy use medical robots for COVID-19 identification centres (Romero 2020). They can monitor the temperature of patients as well as offer medications to patients being held in the quarantine. They also disinfect areas. Modern practices significantly reduce the chance of healthcare personnel being infected by the coronavirus. Furthermore, they save safety equipment, such as PPEs, required by staff in close proximity to their patients. Thus, it suggests IoT applications can benefit the healthcare sector in many ways during times of crisis.

Remote Workforce

The COVID-19 outbreak has forced thousands of businesses, organizations and schools to adhere to guidelines on social distancing, and also take on the latest measures for remote and virtual work. This has been a common method of work for the majority of companies since the emergence of coronavirus. There is a good chance that this trend of remote working will not stop up to the announcement of the COVID-19 vaccine.

It is crucial to remember that remote working isn't a new concept. Actually, it's become a trend over long in the past.

Remote work gives greater flexibility for employers as well as employees. Staff members do not have to spend time and energy traveling to work from home. The companies also get the benefit of saving a substantial sum of money on rent and other energy costs.

Additionally, companies are realizing that remote working lets them have multiple staff and teams in various places, which is very beneficial to many companies. There is no doubt that IoT technology is constantly growing in a variety of sectors. In the end, businesses who already implemented effective IoT solutions quickly shifted to remote working.

IoT technology like cloud computing, collaborative software like video conference software, project tools for managing projects, VPN, remote access among others. These tools are in use for quite a while now. However, the recent COVID-19 epidemic has emphasized their significance. In the end, there is a high likelihood that the need for these devices and technologies will rise in the period between the years 2020-2021.

Chapter 10: How The Internet Of Things Is Going To Be In The Near-Term?

Rise of Smart Homes

The idea of smart homes is growing in popularity due to the fact that a number of technology giants are working on intelligent home technologies and gadgets. The industry is led by Google as well as Amazon. In the past few years, a number of companies have emerged from the industry of smart home.

Modern technology is connected to every device and gadget is used every day, such as tablets, smartphones as well as laptops, computers and many other equipments such as complex windows blinds, irrigation systems lighting as well as smart thermostats and numerous other devices that are technologically advanced. In the course of time, major advancements are being made to the IT sector, and a variety of new gadgets are coming out each day.

Experts believe that we're close to huge growth in people taking on the idea that smart home technology is coming to the market. The Intel survey indicates that consumers anticipate seeing at the very least one smart home gadget for every house in 2025 (Intel 2020).

In addition, various surveys have shown the smart home contributes an enormous amount of cash in the total worth of the IoT sector. Based on Guidehouse Insights, smart home IoT devices' worldwide market is projected to experience a massive growth by 18% from 2020-2029 (Smart Energy International 2020).

The COVID-19 epidemic has harmed the expansion of the smart home device market. In the meantime the public is becoming drawn to products for smart homes that can improve the fitness and health of individuals. As a result, there are likely to be many shifts regarding this.

Benefits of a Smart Home

There are many benefits of changing your home to smart homes. A few of them (Sublime Technologies 2018, 2018):

The technology industry is changing every day. If you'd like to keep on top of the current trends and make the most of advanced tools and technologies accessible worldwide, you ought be thinking about having an intelligent home. There is no doubt that smart homes aren't a luxury that is only available to the wealthy. They have now become necessary to live contemporary lifestyles.

Smart homes play an essential part in improving efficiency overall and the quality of our daily lives. It is easy to control a variety of devices and systems using one touch or a voice commands. You can, for instance, make use of the device's smart features to control the heating system or the overall air conditioning system within your home. Other functions such as changing the on/off of lights in a single touch can also boost the efficiency of your home and reduces the use of power.

In addition to a higher level of productivity, smart homes can also provide greater convenience and ease into your life. It is not necessary to leave your home to accomplish routine tasks. Instead, you'll be able to operate them from your smartphone as it lets you conduct every essential task in your household using numerous apps.

Smart homes are also a tranquility because you can utilize these gadgets to keep an eye on windows, doors and various kinds of sensors. Also, you can examine the garage door from at-home comforts of your home to make sure it's properly shut, without having to go outside.

It is no secret that people like customization And one among the greatest advantages of smart houses is that they can be highly customized. It is possible to set a certain period for drawing the shades. Furthermore, you could use apps to alter the intensity of both indoor and outdoor lighting. Other electronic devices are easy to regulate and personalized in a smart well-planned smart home.

A further reason to transform your home to smart homes is that it plays crucial roles in green living and sustainable development. If you are able to control the lighting fixtures using your phone and reduce their brightness or switch them off when needed. This means you'll be reducing electricity consumption and reducing the expense of power.

Smart power strips can help users to save an enormous amount of cash by shutting off appliances that aren't in use. Smart thermostats also have the capability to automatically adjust the temperature depending on the outdoor climate. Smart toilets are also designed to reduce the use of water.

It is a given it is true that smart houses are more secure and safer than conventional home setups. It is easy to turn on or off intelligent security devices in only a couple of seconds using applications that are available on mobile phones. Therefore, if in the outdoors and forget to shut every appliance off it is not necessary to fret about it since you are able to do this on your phone.

Applications of IoT in the Automotive Industry

IoT can be used in any business sector, not just the industry of automation and transportation. Smart cars' fame is growing rapidly because consumers want to find new and more efficient ways to travel. Furthermore, the intelligent transportation system is an integral part of any city that is smart. Leading global automobile makers are aware of these needs, and an enormous portion of the budget is devoted for research and development smart vehicles and other similar technologies (Keertikumar Malagund, 2015).

The annual output of the automotive industry is thought at 70- 800 million pieces. It's one of the biggest manufacturing industries around the world. In addition, statistics from around the world show that the automobile industry in the world is worth $3 trillion dollars.

It does however suggest that the automotive industry has not been confronted with the same set of problems. According to the statistics, car sales have fluctuated between similar levels over the last four years. The result is that the business has not been increasing (Biz4Intellia 2020). The main reason why the auto industry does not grow is the absence of advanced technologies in most cars.

There are a few automobile manufacturers and top businesses are focused on the development of innovative technologies in the sector. In contrast customers are looking for a car that offers significantly more than merely four wheels and a wheel. The demand for vehicles that be connected and interconnected is increasing in a continuous manner.

So IoT Internet of Things is playing crucial roles to help the automotive sector meet the demands of customers with cutting-edge vehicles. The advent of IoT within the automotive business has provided possibilities for producers and buyers around the globe. IoT can be used at the individual, industrial as well as commercial scales. It is now a favored location for the latest all-in-one and modern-day solutions.

There are numerous applications of IoT for the automobile business because firms develop and release various kinds of autonomous vehicles. The following are the most prominent four examples of IoT within the automobile industry (Biz4Intellia 2020):

Fleet Management

The advent of IoT within the automotive sector has led to a number of new developments in the area of management of fleets. Large vehicles, such as trucks, have been incorporated with GPS devices for location such as weight measurement as well as other sensors similar to. These sensors' purpose is to gather details from the vehicle as well as compile accurate and thorough reports.

Most of the time, data like this is saved directly to an effective cloud-based computing platform. It is then analysed and processed by right analytical tools capable of transforming data in a visual format. In the end, an operator of a fleet can comprehend and read this data for regulating various parameters that are associated to the fleet.

Smart Cars

There is no doubt to state that autonomous vehicles also known as smart cars, are currently the top of the line for automobile manufacturers. A lot of car companies are creating fully automated vehicles which are able to handle every aspect of driving inside a vehicle. Although many advances have been achieved in this field but there's still much work to complete as a fully automated car has yet to be made available for public consumption.

Yet, intelligent cars equipped with semi-automated features to assist motorists in tasks such as stopping, driving and parking are currently available in the marketplace. These cars were developed by using IoT technology. These cars can make accurate decisions when partially controlling the operation of vehicles. There is evidence that smart cars are essential to the prevention of road accidents since they lessen the load on the driver. Smart vehicles are connected to diverse IoT technology to limit human error, and help enhance the driving experience to make it safer, more enjoyable and relaxing.

Efficient Maintenance System

Predictive analytics is among the most well-known applications of IoT technology in a variety of industries which includes automotive. IoT permits various sensors to integrate into the various parts of cars. The sensors can be capable of collecting information and sharing that data on an appropriate platform. The information is then processed using reliable algorithms to ensure accurate analysis as well as predicting potential results based upon the different elements' capabilities.

It's clear that IoT applications have changed the IoT automated maintenance and procedures because users are aware of likely issues that may cause unexpected breakdowns. Similar to the dashboard indicator in a car, which alert drivers to potential issues.

But, with IoT technologies, motorists get access to more in-depth analyses since the data can be sent straight to their smartphone, long prior to the issue forming. This means that drivers can take the right decision on how to get the vehicle repaired. This helps to save costs and time since the motorist will not need the burden of a catastrophic malfunctioning component while driving.

Many features of predictive maintenance can be implemented on personal automobiles as well as vast fleet of vehicles. The technology is extremely advantageous when it comes to heavy vehicles such as the ones that carry loads. They often have to travel for days or weeks prior to arriving at their final destination. Thus, using modern-day maintenance tools made available via IoT technology, individuals are able to evaluate the performance of their vehicles and make repairs before they begin to malfunction.

Connected Cars

The connected car is also a smart vehicles that have been around for quite a long the past few years. Indeed, a study suggests that we could have around 250 million connected vehicles at the end of 2021 (Biz4Intellia 2020). There are a variety of IoT technology and protocols that are involved with these kinds of intelligent vehicles. R

In general, vehicles are linked to an IoT network known as cellular that connects to all systems (CV2X) that connects vehicles as well as smart transportation devices. The advantage of connected vehicles is the ability to provide speedy data transmission as well as increase drivers' speed of response through better car communication.

CV2X can be divided into four different categories:

V2V (short for Vehicle to Car) (V2V) connections permit vehicles within a certain distance to communicate with each the other. This data typically focuses on details related to velocity, dynamic, as well as locations. These connections can to prevent accidents as well as allow emergency vehicles such as ambulances and trucks to navigate through congestion.

Connection of the vehicle to the infrastructure (V2I) connectivity refers to the network of vehicles as well as the infrastructures surrounding them, such as traffic signals, lane markings as well as booths. It facilitates the flow of traffic and reduces queues at petrol stations and toll booths.

Connections between pedestrians and vehicles (V2P) connections means that pedestrians may also be connected to CV2X through the use of mobile applications. This application's purpose is to enable users to find taxis that are in the vicinity and to track the approximate date of the arrival of the vehicles they have requested. They also can be connected to the pedestrian-friendly walking system, and alter the signal for crossing the street.

Vehicle to Network (V2N) is the process of connecting the smart transport system with weather forecast departments to inform the motorists about potential drastic shifts in weather conditions. Additionally, information on road accidents are also made available to motorists. The smartphone users are able to connect to their vehicle using V2N. This means that users can make use of voice commands to access the music system as well as GPS of the vehicle when driving.

Rise of Smart Cities

A variety of property developers, businesses as well as government agencies as well as investors from all over the world have been working hard to create state-of-the-art advancements under smart city programs. The goal of these measures and initiatives is to make cities more sustainable, efficient as well as appealing to residents and investors. They also help boost economic growth in current time.

There are many issues in implementing these plans since each and every city in the world has its own uniqueness and particular characteristics. There isn't any one universal strategy for transforming the city to one that is smart. But, as time passes many smart city options have become well-liked in a variety of nations. The most common elements in developing the smart city include adopting the best practices for funding and design, and use of IoT technology.

Features of Smart Cities

The most effective way to describe an intelligent city is to track and incorporate diverse conditions across all the crucial infrastructures such as bridges, roads tunnels, railway lines and airports, communications, power supply, and structures. Through these measures smart cities can improve its resource utilization and devise strategies to maintain the facilities and make cities more safe and secure through the easy monitoring of different security elements.

Smart cities also come with robust emergency response systems that can respond immediately to man-made and natural disasters. These systems are built for rapid response to make the appropriate decisions before any catastrophe hits the city. Advanced monitoring systems come with integrated smart sensors that can collect details and then analyze them immediately. This enhances the capacity of municipal management (Hall 2000).)

Components of a Smart City

Smart cities that are well designed and planned made up of various of technological and modern tools. A smart city should consist of smart homes as well as smart energy, intelligent transport systems, smart energy systems, intelligent water management as well as other smart technology systems that can revolutionize society and permit the utilization of technology that connects the physical and digital worlds.

The fundamental building block for all these technology is information and communications technology (ICT) as well as the Internet of Things. These technologies form the basis of infrastructure that includes actuators, sensors, as well as advanced and sophisticated electronic devices like cloud computing, large data analysis tools, as well as the mobile edge computing devices. Without IoT the above innovations would have been feasible initially.

When these systems are effectively integrated into a smart city project, they could be fully autonomous, interoperable secure, and reliable. The communications between the various devices and their connections is strongly dependent upon the communication gateway which connects the electronics and sensors to the Internet to improve administration and control of intelligent technology.

General Model of a Smart City

The traditional Smart City design, subsystems communicate together using high-quality telecommunications and data technology. Additionally, the city is divided into an constructed environment, which includes homes buildings, offices, stores, and a myriad of other equipment. It also encompasses the infrastructure-based industries like energy as well as services-related industries such as healthcare and education. The systems and the industries need to connect with one with respect to one way or the other since the main function of a smart town is to improve connectivity and enable the various subsystems to work together (Imperial College London, 2019,).

By implementing IoT technologies as well as modern technologies, a city is able to have maximum connectivity with vital sectors such as communications, information technology and electronic devices. Smart cities' main focus is utilizing sensors to gather information from various parts in the town. The data collected is then compiled with other data, stored, analysed, and presented in a manner that is appropriate. Additionally, data analyses are usually the foundation of crucial decision-making to tackle diverse issues and trends.

Importance of Smart Cities

There is no surprise to see that more nations are beginning to be interested in the development of intelligent cities. Popularity of these cities is growing among the populous and also. The primary reason behind this is because the key to a smart city is linking and integration of complex technologies, and is a sustainable, human-centered model which expands the application of technology for communication for transforming people's lives in a positive way.

Smart cities make use of the new-age ecology of cities, and the latest technologies such as IoT solutions as well as cloud computing solutions Big Data Analysis and the interaction of humans with machines, infrastructure and the entire environment using different protocols and tools. The result is that it significantly improves the quality of life for citizens and provides viable economic opportunities for development by drawing investors from across the globe (Benetyte (2013)).

Home-Based Appliances

A smart home is the blend of a variety of smart home appliances that connect to the Internet using the appropriate IoT technology. There's a huge list of appliances that are home-based in which IoT is utilized. There are a few examples:

Smart Cookware

Smart cookware is a wide variety of kitchen appliances that operate with intelligent controls via Wi-Fi. The smart cookware is a great choice to cook any meal and are therefore an integral part of any smart home. One interesting aspect of the smart cookware is that these appliances were first introduced some time long ago. Basic devices such as pots that have a timers and other gadgets that regulate cooking are intelligent cookware.

Thanks to the growth of Internet and IoT There are nearly unlimited options to cook with intelligent cookware. It is evident that IoT has changed how we cook and consume food. It is possible to use the smart cookware to accomplish a variety of tasks, such as searching at recipes via the Internet or controlling your oven using your smartphone as well as weighing the calories as well as managing your diet overall.

Smart TVs

The advent of smart TVs can be a common application for the Internet of Things. Most of the current television models are compatible with ethernet and Wi-Fi connectivity, which has created many possibilities. This means that smart TVs can be connected to the home network to give users with access to everything and everything that is available through the Internet. Televisions are also capable of being connected to the Internet for the purpose of offering OTT services, or streaming services, such as Netflix for the viewers. These kinds of apps illustrate the fact that IoT has truly transformed the television industry.

Smart Speakers

The smart speakers are considered to be the mainstay of smart home because they are able to manage almost any other electronic device in a home. They have a wide range of possibilities of connectivity. They are able to benefit from the benefits of both AI and cloud system's advantages to work with many IoT gadgets. Smart speakers' primary attributes and advantages comprise voice-based controls for music playback, controlling the home's smarts messages, as well as inquiries about information. They can also be the perfect audio source for your smart home and can provide doorsbell chimes, alerts, alarms, as well as a host of additional features.

Chapter 11: Security Issues Of The Iot

Every statistic and current trends show that the Internet of Things industry is constantly growing in a rapid manner. The IoT technology and industry have led to a major change for both professional and private lives, as IoT uses in almost every other sector. Furthermore, the applications of IoT have not been only for humans, since it is now a necessity to the success of implementing numerous machines and smart infrastructure.

In the preceding chapter, IoT has numerous advantages. But, as with other areas of technology There are certain issues as well as security dangers that are related to IoT and other technologies. One of the main reasons for these risks is because technology, particularly security system, hasn't developed enough, meaning that IoT isn't completely secure and secure.

The entire IoT infrastructure is made up of a variety of factors like users, manufacturers as well as protocols for interaction to the network infrastructure. In the end, there are numerous security issues during the development of IoT technology. IoT is very appealing for consumers because they are eager to use it both in their the professional and personal lives. But, it can also lead people to embrace the latest tools and technologies to make use of the technology prior to implementing the safety protocols that are essential.

Here are a few of the most significant security risks associated with IoT:

Security Risks in Smart Homes

There could be a myriad of security concerns for smart homes since they make use of a wide range of IoT technology with its unique set of security dangers. One of the most prevalent instances of IoT security concerns with Smart houses is the threat of home intrusion because the modern technology blurs the lines between physical and virtual realms. In the end, IoT people are vulnerable to dangerous dangers.

Furthermore, home automation raises the chance of having the security of your personal information being compromised by cyber criminals particularly if the devices you use have security issues and appropriate methods aren't in place. When the IP addresses for smart homes have been exposed, hackers could make use of them to track the address of users. There's no limit to the possibility of using this technique since the addresses of users may even be used to access the inner criminal networks. One common approach to avoiding this kind of issue as well as IoT security breaches is to use VPNs and secure authentication credentials for logins.

Home owners who have smart devices are also at greater chance of being a victim of identity theft since when a cyber-attacker is able to enter your home remotely and gain access to all your smart devices as well as private information. Thus, hackers could access the databases of the devices' business to collect vital information. If this happens the cybercriminals could gain access to your credit card as well as other sensitive information that is why you could end up being a victim identity theft criminal.

Unencrypted Communication

A study in 2019 carried out by the world's leading IT security company called Zscaler has revealed that 91.5 percent of IoT communication within large companies were conducted on unencrypted wireless networks, which makes them susceptible to interference of all kinds. Based on this research the companies handled thousands of transactions and the majority of them did not have any encryption at all, which made the information vulnerable to being hacked or altered by hackers (Greene 2019.).

The study revealed a variety of realisations about why even the largest corporations and multinational companies aren't implementing the needed security tools. IoT devices are able to leave a large digital footprint that makes it easy for cyber criminals to monitor different types of functions and transactions on unsecure Wi-Fi.

Application of RFID

Radio Frequency Identification (RFID) is a technology that makes use of radio waves for the transmission of data and communications between an individual system as well as an item. The uses of RFID technology within the IoT sector are widespread and range across. RFID tags are utilized for daily communication between items and the hubs that are primary. Similar to the healthcare business, RFID tags are attached to medical equipment that is mobile.

These kinds of capabilities make RFID an important element in the IoT system. Simply put, RFID is essential in IoT to join a variety of items to the network as well as to allow them to grow and transmit information.

The Hijacking of IoT Devices

IoT devices usually come with a weak security system. In turn, these devices are more susceptible to ransomware, as well as other kinds of cyber-attacks. It is the type of malware that blocks the access to data and prevents users from gaining access to their files until certain conditions are met. Most often, cybercriminals will demand ransom in order to recover their data.

www.ingramcontent.com/pod-product-compliance
Lightning Source LLC
LaVergne TN
LVHW022315060326

832902LV00020B/3475